EXOPLANETS

WORLDS BEYOND OUR SOLAR SYSTEM

To my favorite star watcher, Nicholson Kenney

Twenty-First Century Books
A division of Lerner Publishing Group, Inc.
241 First Avenue North
Minneapolis, MN 55401 USA

For reading levels and more information, look up this title at www.lernerbooks.com.

Main body text set in Adobe Garamond Pro 11/15
Typeface provided by Adobe Systems.

Library of Congress Cataloging-in-Publication Data

Names: Kenney, Karen Latchana.
Title: Exoplanets / by Karen Latchana Kenney.
Description: Minneapolis : Twenty-First Century Books, [2017] | Audience: Age 13–18. |
    Audience: Grade 9 to 12. | Includes bibliographical references and index.
Identifiers: LCCN 2016010442 (print) | LCCN 2016020089 (ebook) | ISBN 9781512400861
    (lb : alk. paper) | ISBN 9781512428490 (eb pdf)
Subjects: LCSH: Extrasolar planets—Juvenile literature. | Planets—Juvenile literature. |
    Milky Way—Juvenile literature.
Classification: LCC QB820 .K46 2017 (print) | LCC QB820 (ebook) | DDC 523.2/4—dc23

LC record available at https://lccn.loc.gov/2016010442

Manufactured in the United States of America
1-38930-20905-8/8/2016

CONTENTS

CHAPTER 1

INTO THE MILKY WAY

An artist's rendering shows the planet 51 Peg b crossing its parent star, as seen from the surface of a moon.

Our sun is but one of many stars. We know that every star has at least one planet. . . . Our night sky is literally teeming with exoplanets.

—Sara Seager, astrophysicist, Massachusetts Institute of Technology, 2015

It was October 5, 1995—a day that Swiss astronomers Michel Mayor and Didier Queloz had been excitedly waiting for. The two scientists had big news to share at a conference on sunlike stars in Florence, Italy. Until then, Mayor and Queloz had kept their news a secret, sharing it with only a few close colleagues and journal editors.

At the Haute-Provence Observatory in France, Mayor and Queloz had been working at the Élodie spectrograph, an instrument used to study light traveling through space. One sunlike star they studied with the spectrograph—a star called 51 Peg (short for 51 Pegasus), found in a group of stars known as the Pegasus constellation—was particularly interesting. What its light revealed would soon rock the scientific community.

The two scientists had discovered a planet orbiting 51 Peg. Called 51 Peg b, it was the first exoplanet (planet outside our solar system) orbiting a sunlike star that scientists had ever found. Mayor and Queloz had detected a wobbling motion in the star. The wobble showed that something was pulling on it.

Gravity is a force that attracts objects in the universe to one another. A star's gravity keeps planets orbiting, or circling, the star. But planets also pull on their stars and other objects in space. In a solar system, this pull makes the star wobble a little.

This illustration shows the exoplanet 51 Peg b (*left*) and its star, 51 Peg. The planet's discovery in 1994 was a breakthrough, because astronomers had never before found a planet orbiting a sunlike star.

Mayor and Queloz had used 51 Peg's wobble to deduce the size of 51 Peg b and to determine how long it took the planet to orbit the star. They used other calculations to determine what the planet was made of.

AN UNUSUAL PLANET

The planet that was pulling on 51 Peg was unusual—unlike any planet scientists had ever seen. The astronomers' calculations had revealed that the planet was a gas giant, a massive planet made mostly of gas, with an icy core at its center. It was as large as or larger than our solar system's Jupiter, a planet so big that close to thirteen hundred Earths could fit inside it. Yet 51 Peg b's location was odd. It orbited very close to its star.

Most scientists then believed that gas giants had to orbit far away from stars, where temperatures are colder. Scientists thought that areas close to stars were too hot for planets with icy cores. But the newly discovered exoplanet was a mere 5 million miles (8 million kilometers) away from its star. Compared with Earth, which sits 93 million miles (150 million km) away from the sun, 51 Peg b was practically on top of its star. In addition, it orbited its star in just a little more than 4 days, compared to 365 days for Earth.

The exoplanet was so unusual that Mayor and Queloz waited a full year, verifying their measurements before announcing their discovery. They had discovered the star's back-and-forth motion, indicating the gravitational pull of an orbiting planet, in 1994. The scientists returned to the Haute-Provence Observatory and measured 51 Peg a second time in July 1995.

The new data they recorded matched their previous results, showing that their measurements were correct. They concluded that this large planet had formed farther away from its star but had then migrated toward it. With this explanation, Mayor and Queloz submitted their explosive research article titled "A Jupiter-Mass Companion to a Solar-Type Star" to the journal *Nature* in August 1995. It was accepted for publication just before the conference in Florence.

BREAKING THE NEWS

Despite Mayor and Queloz having kept the news relatively secret, word was out and the astronomical community buzzed with excitement. When Mayor arrived in Florence, faxes from reporters requesting interviews had piled up at his hotel. His forty-five-minute presentation on the discovery of 51 Peg b ended with the audience's applause, but that didn't mean everyone was convinced. According to Mayor, "Some people at the meeting were really intrigued," but they wanted to figure out why the planet had such a short orbit.

Swiss astronomers Didier Queloz (*left*) and Michel Mayor (*right*) discovered Peg 51 b. Here they hold the 1995 issue of *Nature* that published their findings about the exoplanet.

Others questioned the findings, telling Mayor and Queloz, "You don't have enough precision [in your measurements]."

After the exoplanet news broke, it needed verification by a separate team of scientists for the scientific community to accept the data. Astronomers Geoffrey Marcy and Paul Butler accepted the challenge. They made their observations at the University of California's Lick Observatory and soon had their results. Marcy wrote to Mayor: "We have obtained 27 observations of 51 Peg, covering 4 days. . . . We find [an orbit] of 4.2 days. . . . So your wonderful discovery is confirmed!!! Congratulations again!"

It was official. Scientists finally had proof that our solar system was not unique. If we could find one exoplanet orbiting a sunlike star, how many more could we find? And of those planets, was it possible that some supported life?

HOT, COLD, AND SUPER · · · · · · · · · · · · ·

Astronomers categorize exoplanets by comparing them to planets in our solar system. For instance, planets called hot Jupiters, such as 51 Peg b, are gas giants (like Jupiter) that orbit close to their stars, in the hottest parts of their solar systems. Cold Jupiters are gas giants that orbit farther away from their stars, in cold parts of their solar systems. Super-Earths are about ten times the size of Earth (much smaller than gas giants). They can be made of gas, rock, or both. A hot Neptune is a planet that is between ten and twenty times the size of Earth—close in size to Neptune or Uranus—but that orbits very close to its star, closer than Mercury is to the sun in our solar system. A pulsar planet is one that orbits around a pulsar, or a rapidly spinning star. Some exoplanets are even rogue planets. They wander through space, unattached to stars.

STUDYING THE STARS

Getting to the first exoplanet discovery was a long and often controversial journey—one that had begun ages before, when we humans first wondered about our place in the solar system and the universe. The sun illuminates and colors our world by day. It warms us and provides energy for the growth of plants, which give us food. But the night sky reveals much more than the daytime sky. It holds a multitude of bright pinpoints beaming across the blackness, showing a glimpse of the crowded cosmos beyond our solar system. Out there in deep space, stars fill our galaxy, a galaxy called the Milky Way. It is home to billions of stars and solar systems, all spinning as a group and held together by gravity.

THE BIRTH OF A SOLAR SYSTEM

A solar system starts taking shape in a nebula, a swirling cloud of gas and dust adrift in space. The gas and dust turn into a flat, spinning disk with a dense, hot core. The core gets hotter and bigger and becomes a star.

Dust in the disk starts clumping together as well, still spinning around the star. The clumps grow larger and larger over billions of years, swallowing whatever lies in their paths. The clumps become planets and their moons, all pulled into orbit by their star's gravity. Together, all the swirling objects form a solar system.

Ancient peoples observed and recorded the positions of stars as early as 1600 BCE. That's when ancient astronomers created the Nebra sky disk. Named for the German town where it was found in the late twentieth century, the disk is the oldest known map of the night sky. The bronze disk, which measures 13 inches (32 centimeters) across, is adorned with gold shapes representing celestial objects, believed to be the moon, the sun, and the Pleiades star cluster.

The ancient Greek astronomer Ptolemy believed that the sun, stars, and planets revolved around Earth. This image from *Harmonia Macrocosmica*, an atlas of the stars published in Holland in 1660, shows Ptolemy's view. But the atlas also included the ideas of later astronomers, such as Nicolaus Copernicus. In the early 1500s, Copernicus said that Earth and the other planets revolved around the sun.

Astronomers in Babylon, an ancient city in the Middle East, studied constellations in the night sky. The ancient Greeks also studied constellations, and Greek scientists used geometry to estimate Earth's size. The ancient Greek astronomers Hipparchus and Ptolemy studied planetary motion. Around 150 CE, Ptolemy wrote a manuscript called the *Almagest*, which described his model of the universe. Ptolemy asserted that Earth was at the center of the universe, with the sun, other planets, and stars orbiting it. This geocentric (Earth-centered) theory remained the predominant view of the universe for the next fourteen hundred years.

Starting in the eighth century CE, astronomers in the Middle East studied the *Almagest* and worked to improve upon Ptolemy's theories. In Europe, however, the study of astronomy came to a near standstill in the

Middle Ages (about 500–1500). Still, some Europeans wondered about exoplanets. Albert the Great, a thirteenth-century German Catholic bishop, wrote, "Do there exist many worlds or does only one exist? This question is without a doubt one of the most noble and exalting questions raised by the study of Nature."

The first astronomer to challenge the geocentric theory was Nicolaus Copernicus of Poland. In the early sixteenth century, he proposed instead a heliocentric (sun-centered) theory—the idea that Earth and other planets orbited the sun. This was a radical idea at the time. Not only had astronomers believed in the geocentric theory for almost one thousand years, but the Catholic Church, a powerful force in Europe, also backed this theory. The church based its stance on biblical passages that asserted that Earth was at the center of the universe. Proposing ideas that challenged church doctrine was dangerous in this era, because the church often punished those who questioned its teachings. But while Copernicus's heliocentric theory was controversial, many astronomers accepted it.

Danish astronomer Tycho Brahe (1546–1601) did not completely accept the heliocentric view. Like Ptolemy, he believed that Earth was at the universe's center. But he had studied the planets visually and made measurements with early astronomical devices. His studies had shown that the other planets did not orbit Earth. He proposed a hybrid view, stating that while the sun and moon orbited Earth, other planets in our solar system orbited the sun.

One avid supporter of the heliocentric theory was Italian friar and philosopher Giordano Bruno. In the sixteenth century, he proposed that God had created an infinite universe holding many sunlike stars and Earthlike planets. He wrote, "It is thus that the excellence of God is amplified and manifested by the greatness of his empire. It is not glorified just by one, but by countless Suns, not by just one Earth and a world, but by thousands of thousands, what am I saying? an infinity [of worlds]."

In 1597 the Catholic Church asked Bruno to renounce his views on the existence of many worlds. Bruno refused, and Pope Clement VIII, the leader of the church, ordered his execution. Bruno was burned at the stake on February 17, 1600.

Astronomers continued to study the solar system, despite church opposition. Another supporter of the heliocentric theory was Johannes Kepler. This German mathematics teacher published three laws of planetary motion in the early seventeenth century. His observations helped scientists better understand how a solar system works.

BIRTH OF THE TELESCOPE

In 1608 seeing into the universe became much easier. That's when someone in Europe, possibly Dutch optician Hans Lippershey (although historians aren't sure), made the first telescope. A device consisting of two glass lenses inside a tube, a telescope magnifies images of distant objects. A year later, Italian astronomer Galileo Galilei improved on the original telescope design. He figured out how to best shape the lenses and used mathematics to determine how far they needed to be from each other to increase magnification. By the late fall of 1609, he had built a telescope that could make objects appear to be twenty times their normal size. Galileo used his new telescope to observe Mars. Further improvements enabled people to use telescopes to view other planets in our solar system.

The church continued to oppose the heliocentric theory, and in 1633, a church court sentenced Galileo to life imprisonment for promoting this theory. But gradually the church dropped its opposition to new theories about the universe, and scientific inquiry continued to advance. In 1687 English scientist Isaac Newton combined Kepler's and Galileo's ideas about planetary motion. These ideas led him to his universal law of gravitation, which explained how gravity worked. Newton's ideas about gravity explained why objects fall to Earth's surface and why Earth orbits the sun.

Dutch astronomer Christiaan Huygens also studied Mars with a telescope. He wondered about exoplanets and extraterrestrial life (life beyond Earth). In his 1689 book *Cosmotheros*, he wrote, "The nature of the stars and that of the Sun is the same. Which implies a conception of the world much more grandiose than that which corresponds to previous . . . traditional views. . . . What stops us now from thinking that each of these stars or Suns has Planets around it?"

In the mid-eighteenth century, English astronomer Thomas Wright also wondered about the nature of the universe. His view of an infinite cosmos led German scientist and philosopher Immanuel Kant to theorize that our solar system was part of a larger galaxy. Our view of the universe was expanding. What more could be discovered with better technology?

OUR SOLAR-SYSTEM

Kuiper Belt
Pluto
Neptune
Uranus
Saturn
Jupiter
asteroid belt
Sun
Mars
Earth
Venus
Mercury

Our solar system holds eight full-size planets and the dwarf planet Pluto. A large belt of asteroids circles the sun between Mars and Jupiter. Dwarf planets and other small objects travel in the Kuiper Belt beyond Pluto.

NEW PLANETS, NEW DISCOVERIES

From ancient times, people knew about Mercury, Venus, Mars, Jupiter, and Saturn—planets that can be seen with the naked eye. But telescopes enabled people to discover planets never known before. With his self-made telescope, British astronomer William Herschel found the distant planet Uranus in 1781. Even farther out was Neptune. At first, astronomers only guessed at its existence because they believed that the gravity of a distant planet was pulling on Uranus. Using calculations provided by other European scientists, German astronomer Johann Galle located Neptune with a telescope in 1846. In 1930 apprentice US telescope operator Clyde Tombaugh found Pluto, which was then thought to be the farthest planet from the sun. (In 2006 the International Astronomical Union, a group in charge of naming celestial bodies, reclassified Pluto. It became a dwarf planet because of its small size.)

Humans had mapped the solar system and had begun to look beyond it. In the 1910s, at the Mount Wilson Observatory in California, US scientist Harlow Shapley used a telescope measuring 60 inches (152 cm) across to observe the Milky Way. He calculated that the sun sat 50,000 light-years away from the center of the galaxy, a figure that was later revised to 30,000 light-years. (One light-year is the distance that light, which moves at 186,000 miles [300,000 km] per second, can travel in a year.) Shapley's work showed that our solar system is about halfway between the center and the edge of our galaxy. He also observed many cloudlike nebulae, or star-forming dust clouds, and believed that they all existed within the Milky Way. Shapley and many other scientists of this era believed that the universe held only one galaxy.

US scientist Edwin Hubble studied nebulae too, but he believed that some of them existed outside the Milky Way. He carefully photographed the Andromeda galaxy. At the time, it was thought to be a nebula within the Milky Way. In Andromeda, he saw a star called a Cepheid variable. This kind of star has a pulsating light. Scientists had previously figured out how to measure the distance of a Cepheid variable from Earth by analyzing its varying brightness. Hubble used the Cepheid variable he had located to calculate that the Andromeda galaxy was well outside the Milky Way—more than 2 million light-years away. This work proved that other galaxies existed beyond the Milky Way.

Throughout the twentieth century, Hubble and other scientists continued finding more galaxies. It became clear that our solar system was

Working at the Mount Wilson Observatory in California, US astronomer Edwin Hubble proved that the Milky Way is not the only galaxy in the universe.

probably not unique. British astrophysicist Stephen Hawking later said, "The earth is a medium-sized planet orbiting around an average star in the outer suburbs of an ordinary spiral galaxy, which is itself only one of about a million million galaxies in the observable universe."

EXOPLANETS EVERYWHERE

During the twentieth century, engineers developed more powerful telescopes. These included not only telescopes that magnified visual images but also those that detected radio waves. Using a radio telescope, in

1992 astronomers Aleksander Wolszczan of Poland and Dale Frail of Canada discovered three exoplanets—the first ever found. These rocky planets orbit a pulsar, which is a rapidly spinning, dying star that emits radiation in the form of radio waves. The powerful beams of radiation emitted by pulsars make any orbiting planets inhospitable to life. In 1993 astronomers discovered another exoplanet. It travels a one-hundred-year orbit around a binary star system (a solar system with two stars at its center). One star in the system is a pulsar, and the other is a white dwarf, a star that has run out of fuel. Then, in 1994, Mayor and Queloz found 51 Peg b orbiting a sunlike star. This discovery opened up the possibility of finding a solar system like our own, the only solar system known to have life.

The Chandra X-ray Observatory, an orbiting X-ray telescope, captured this image of a nebula, an area in space where stars are forming.

Since the mid-1990s, astronomers have found many more exoplanets. As of May 2016, the National Aeronautics and Space Administration (NASA, the US space agency) had confirmed the existence of 3,264 exoplanets, with more than 4,000 other possible exoplanets being examined.

Some of these planets are in what scientists call the Goldilocks zone, which is a habitable zone. The Goldilocks zone is a planetary orbit around a star that is not too hot (too close to the star) or too cold (too far from the star) for water to exist in a liquid state. The zone is "just right"—as the little girl in the fairy tale "Goldilocks and the Three Bears" would say. In that zone, a planet could possibly support liquid water, and scientists say that planets that contain water might be able to support life.

As astronomers continue to improve exoplanet detection methods, the universe continues to unveil its densely populated terrain. One day we may even find life beyond our solar system.

MULTICOLORED STARS ································

Stars are massive fuel-consuming systems with incredibly dense and hot cores. Look up at the sky and you'll see they have different colors, depending on their size and ages.

Our star, the sun, is a midsize yellow star in the middle of its life. Like other stars, it burns the hydrogen inside its core. It will continue to do so for about ten million more years. After all the hydrogen has been consumed, the sun will begin burning the helium in its core. It will also grow larger—so big that it might engulf all the planets in the solar system. As the sun expands, it will turn from yellow to red. It will become a red giant. Finally, when all the helium is gone, the sun will shed its outer layers. It will become a small and very dense white dwarf. In total, our sun will have a life span of about thirteen billion years.

Massive stars, ten times larger than our sun, have shorter lives (about one hundred million years), but they burn through many more stages. For most of their lives, they are blue. After consuming all their hydrogen, they turn red. They go on to consume their helium, oxygen, silicon, and iron. When all this is gone, the massive star becomes a supernova, shooting its outer layers into space at superfast speeds. Its core becomes more and more dense, and it turns into either a light-swallowing black hole or a rapidly spinning neutron star.

A red dwarf, the most common kind of star, is the smallest—about one-tenth to one-half the size of our sun. Red dwarfs live the longest of all stars—up to several trillion years. These stars burn cooler than the sun, making them less bright. When a red dwarf has burned through its supply of hydrogen, it becomes a white dwarf. When all heat has escaped from the star, it turns into a black dwarf.

2 WOBBLES, SHADOWS, BENDS, AND WAVES

The Milky Way holds hundreds of billions of stars, including our sun. It is just one of billions of galaxies in the universe.

From our corner of the cosmos, exoplanets are impossible to see with the naked eye. Planets emit no visible light (although we can sometimes see a sun's light reflecting off them), making them close to invisible against the blackness of space. Yet astronomers have come up with ingenious methods of detecting exoplanets and have even discovered ways to determine what the planets are made of.

Instead of seeing exoplanets directly, scientists use telescopes to find evidence of their existence. This evidence includes radio waves, the bending of a star's light, the gravitational tug of a planet on a star, and shadows created by planets passing in front of stars. On very rare occasions, telescopes have even captured direct images of exoplanets. Studying exoplanets involves astronomical detective work, performed across light-years of space and time.

TRACKING WOBBLES

Although stars appear to be fixed in the sky, they're not. All the stars of the Milky Way (and other galaxies) are part of a rapidly spinning disk. And as it spins, the Milky Way also zooms through space at an incredible 1.3 million miles (2.1 million km) per hour.

Stars don't just move with their galaxies. Stars and whole solar systems also move on their own. This movement, called proper motion, was first identified by British astronomer Edmond Halley in 1718.

He compared star maps from ancient Greece with his own measurements of those same star systems fifteen hundred years later. He found that while many stars were in the same positions shown in the ancient maps, some had moved. His discovery shattered previously accepted views that stars were fixed in space.

Scientists track proper motion using two kinds of measurements. The transverse velocity measurement, made using observations through a telescope, shows how quickly a star is moving sideways as seen from Earth. Radial velocity shows how quickly a star is moving toward or away

MAPPING THE GALAXY · · · · · · · · · · · · · · · · · · ·

Our galaxy, the Milky Way, started to form around thirteen billion years ago and is filled with one hundred to four hundred billion stars. Some of the stars are in the middle of the galaxy, which takes the form of a central bulge. Other stars are in four long curving arms that stretch out from the central bulge. Mapping those stars has long been a goal of scientists.

In 129 BCE, the ancient Greek astronomer Hipparchus made the first catalog of these stars. Modern scientists continue to map these stars to learn about the galaxy's structure, age, and formation and what might be in its future.

In 1989 the European Space Agency (ESA, an organization with twenty-two European member nations) launched a satellite called Hipparcos. The name stood for High Precision Parallax Collecting Satellite and also honored Hipparchus of ancient Greece. The satellite's job was to precisely map more than one hundred thousand stars in the Milky Way using a telescope. After achieving its mission goals, the ESA cut communication with the satellite in 1993.

The ESA Gaia space observatory, a space telescope launched in 2013, aims to map one billion stars in the Milky Way. Gaia is expected to operate for five years and will create a 3-D map of the Milky Way. Scientists believe that Gaia will also discover seven thousand exoplanets using its two telescopes and other equipment.

from us as viewed from Earth. To determine radial velocity, scientists use a spectrometer, a device that measures the light waves emitted by a star. Light in front of a moving object has shorter wavelengths (the distance between two adjacent wave crests), while light behind a moving object has longer wavelengths. By measuring these wavelengths, scientists can tell if a star is moving toward Earth or away from it. With measurements of both transverse and radial velocity, scientists can figure out the true motion of a star.

By taking precise measurements of stars' positions and movements, scientists can detect a star's journey through its galaxy. If astronomers see a zigzag or wobble in that path, they get excited. It could mean that an exoplanet is orbiting that star, pulling on it with its gravity. Larger planets make a bigger wobble in a star's path, while smaller planets pull less on their stars. The bigger wobbles make larger planets easier to find than smaller ones. Looking at the size of the wobble, scientists can also estimate the planet's mass, or amount of matter it contains, which gives them an idea of the star's size.

Canadian astrophysicists Bruce Campbell and Gordon Walker, pioneers in the radial velocity detection method, were the first scientists to observe a wobble in a star's path. Campbell and Walker performed a survey of stars from 1981 to 2002. In 1988 the two scientists announced a probable planet orbiting around a binary star system called Gamma Cephei. The scientists were unsure of their data though. They did additional research and finally, in 2003, announced for certain that a planet was causing the wobble.

US astrophysicist David Latham, working at the Harvard-Smithsonian Center for Astrophysics in Massachusetts, also found a wobble in 1988. The object he had found was HD 114762b, just 90 light-years from Earth. Latham didn't know if HD 114762b was a brown dwarf (an object that forms like a star but doesn't have enough mass to become a star) or a very large hot Jupiter (a gas giant orbiting very close to its star). Latham at first called the object a brown dwarf. Astronomers determined that it was an exoplanet in 2012 and nicknamed it Latham's Planet. The famous 1994 discovery of 51 Peg b was also found through its star's wobble.

Although looking for wobbles was the first successful method of detecting exoplanets, the method can only find large gas giants. It will not likely lead to the discovery of Earthlike planets—small planets with rocky and metal cores. And the method has a limited range. It can't be used to find planets farther than 100 light-years from Earth.

SEEING SHADOWS

Another way to find exoplanets is called the transit detection method. It involves watching for a tiny dimming in a star's brightness. This happens when a planet crosses between our line of sight and its star. The planet makes a shadow on the star, blocking its brightness slightly. The transit detection method has been the most successful yet at finding exoplanets.

To detect transiting planets, scientists gather data about a star's luminosity (brightness) for many years. They may notice a definite drop in a star's luminosity for a certain amount of time. If the drop repeats over regular intervals, it might mean that a planet is orbiting that star.

Smaller planets make smaller shadows, and a star's light dims less than it would with a larger orbiting planet. Knowing this, scientists can deduce a planet's size by measuring the size of the shadow. Often a planet detected by the transit method is confirmed by a radial velocity measurement. It shows if a star is moving slightly due to a planet's gravitational pull. Combined with other information, scientists use the radial velocity measurement to determine a planet's mass. Knowing a planet's size and mass, scientists can then figure out a planet's density. Density is the amount of mass held by an object of a certain size. A measurement of density tells us how compact or airy a planet is. A planet that is very dense might be made from rock. A planet that is less dense might be made from gas.

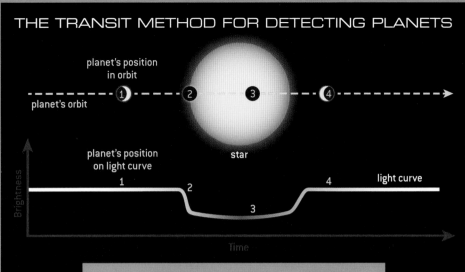

THE TRANSIT METHOD FOR DETECTING PLANETS

planet's position
in orbit

planet's orbit

planet's position
on light curve

star

Brightness

light curve

Time

A temporary dimming in a star's brightness can indicate that a planet is traveling between the star and our line of sight from Earth. Astronomers look for this dimming in the search for exoplanets.

Scientists can also learn about an exoplanet's atmosphere—or the gases surrounding its surface—using the transit method. To do this, they look at how the atmosphere absorbs the star's light. Different gases absorb light of different wavelengths. Scientists see which kinds of light are being absorbed and then make good guesses about gases in the planet's atmosphere. Learning about the atmosphere also tells scientists whether the planet might hold water and how hot or cold its surface temperature gets.

The first exoplanet detected by the transit method was HD 209458b, nicknamed Osiris. Scientists David Charbonneau and Tim Brown at the National Center for Atmospheric Research, a US research agency in Boulder, Colorado, discovered Osiris in 1999. Other scientists confirmed its existence with radial velocity measurements. Scientists learned more about this surprising planet in the following years. Its orbit lasts just three and a half days, and it is very close to its star. Osiris is 1.3 times the size of Jupiter and has a surface temperature of 1,832°F (1,000°C). It has an atmosphere made from sodium, hydrogen, oxygen, and carbon, and this atmosphere

HD 209458b, nicknamed Osiris, was the first exoplanet found using the transit detection method. This illustration from the European Space Agency shows Osiris at the center, its sun in the background, and its long tail of escaping hydrogen gas in blue.

is escaping the planet's gravity. Scientists know this because Osiris has a 125,000-mile (201,000 km) tail of escaping hydrogen gas.

The transit method of exoplanet detection has some problems. First, the orbiting exoplanet has to be within our line of sight for the method to work. So the star, its planet, and Earth all have to be lined up so that the shadow made by the orbiting planet can be seen from Earth. Such an alignment is fairly rare. And this method often leads to false positive results—that is, scientists see dimming, but it turns out to be caused by something other than a planet, such as dust, a star that is dying, or other objects in space. That's why most scientists verify the transit method using a second detection method.

BENDING LIGHT

Sometimes a star's light isn't dimmed by an exoplanet. Instead, an exoplanet might make a star's light appear to momentarily intensify. This intensification occurs during a phenomenon called microlensing. German physicist Albert Einstein first described microlensing in 1916. In his general theory of relativity, Einstein showed that light waves passing by large objects could be bent by the objects' gravity, in the same way that lenses in eyeglasses or a telescope bend light rays that pass through them.

Microlensing sometimes occurs between two stars. Suppose a star comes in between Earth and a distant, bright star. When the stars align, the gravity of the closer star, called the lensing star, bends the light waves of the farther star. The bending creates a bright ring of light called an Einstein ring. If a planet is orbiting the lensing star, it can further intensify light in the Einstein ring. This additional burst of light is a clear sign to astronomers

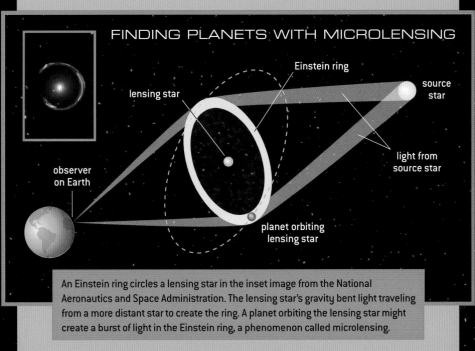

FINDING PLANETS WITH MICROLENSING

Einstein ring

lensing star

source star

observer on Earth

light from source star

planet orbiting lensing star

An Einstein ring circles a lensing star in the inset image from the National Aeronautics and Space Administration. The lensing star's gravity bent light traveling from a more distant star to create the ring. A planet orbiting the lensing star might create a burst of light in the Einstein ring, a phenomenon called microlensing.

of an exoplanet. By analyzing the light with other methods, they can determine the planet's size, mass, and orbit.

This method of detecting exoplanets has advantages over other methods. It can detect planets much farther away than those found by other methods and can find small planets orbiting at great distances from their stars. Scientists David Bennett and Sun Hong Rhie of the University of Notre Dame in Indiana found the first exoplanet using the microlensing method in 1999. The planet, about 20,000 light-years away from the sun, orbited double suns. Astronomers found an even more distant planet—22,000 light-years from Earth—by microlensing in 2006.

A UNIVERSAL BROADCAST

Another way to find exoplanets doesn't rely on visible light. Instead, astronomers search for radio waves broadcast across the universe. The sources of these waves are rapidly spinning, strongly magnetic pulsars, the remnants of exploding stars called supernovas. As it spins, a pulsar beams radiation from its two poles. This radiation hits Earth at regular intervals—so regular that an anomaly (irregularity) is highly noticeable.

Like other stars, a pulsar will wobble if a planet is pulling on it with its gravity. This wobble will affect the regularity of the pulsar's radio signals. On Earth, far from the pulsar, these signal changes are tiny—lasting just fractions of seconds. But by using telescopes that detect radio waves and by collecting data for many years, scientists can detect a planet orbiting a pulsar.

Finding a planet by a pulsar is incredibly rare, however. During the life span of a star, before it reaches the pulsar stage, it grows immensely in size and engulfs nearby planets. When it later explodes in the supernova stage, it ejects outer planets from its gravitational hold. A planet that survives this process is a rare find, and nothing could possibly live on that planet, bathed in its pulsar's deadly radiation.

Still, scientists have found surviving planets around pulsars. In fact, the very first confirmed exoplanets ever found, discovered by Aleksander Wolszczan and Dale Frail in 1992, orbited a pulsar. Wolszczan and Frail found three planets around PSR 1257+12, a pulsar in the Virgo constellation, roughly 890 light-years from Earth. Since then scientists have found only two more exoplanets around pulsars.

THE ELECTROMAGNETIC SPECTRUM · · · · · · · · · ·

Electromagnetic waves are light rays that travel through space at the speed of light. Like waves on the ocean, electromagnetic waves move in undulating (rising and falling) patterns. Also like waves on the ocean, they have crests (peaks) and troughs (valleys). A wavelength is the distance from one crest to the next.

The electromagnetic spectrum is divided into different kinds of waves—gamma rays, X-rays, ultraviolet light, visible light, infrared rays, microwaves, and radio waves. Each kind carries a different kind of energy. Gamma rays have the shortest wavelengths, the fastest vibrations, and the most energy. At the other end of the spectrum, radio waves have the longest wavelengths, the slowest vibrations, and the least energy.

Once astronomers have gathered light waves using telescopes, they use spectrometers to scan, analyze, and record the waves. A machine called a charge-coupled device (CCD) makes a digital image of the spectrum and sends the information to a computer. Scientists can then store and study the digital image.

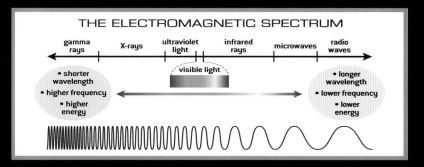

Objects in space emit different types of light rays. Telescopes on land or in space detect and gather incoming rays. Astronomers then scan, analyze, and record the rays using spectrometers and other devices.

This image, captured by a space telescope, shows the Vela pulsar, located about 1,000 light-years from Earth. Pulsars normally emit steady radio signals. Unsteady signals are an indication that a planet's gravity is pulling on a pulsar.

REAL IMAGES

One of the most difficult ways to find exoplanets is through direct imaging—actually seeing a planet visually. This method involves powerful ground-based and space telescopes. Most planets are nearly impossible to see because they do not emit their own light. When we see planets in our own solar system, we are actually seeing the sun's light reflecting off them.

If a planet orbits very close to its star, it cannot be seen in the bright glare of the star's light. If it is very far from its star, the planet will not reflect any of the star's light. To capture a visual image of an exoplanet, it has to be just the right distance from its star to reflect the star's light and in the perfect position for us to see that light from Earth.

Only a few direct images of exoplanets have been made. The first was not actually a planet. It was a brown dwarf imaged by the European

STARLIGHT: TRAVELING BACK IN TIME · · · · · · · ·

When we see starlight, we're not seeing the star as it is at this time. We're seeing an image that began its journey from the star long ago and far away. Light travels 186,000 miles (300,000 km) per second. While that is extremely fast, stars exist billions and trillions of miles from Earth. That means the light we see began traveling many years ago. The star may no longer even exist by the time we see its light. Even the sun's light is delayed because it takes eight minutes to travel from the sun to Earth. So looking at the starlight is like looking back in time and seeing the universe's past.

Southern Observatory's Very Large Telescope (VLT) in Chile in 2004. The VLT is actually a group of four main and four auxiliary telescopes. In addition to detecting visible light, the telescopes can search for infrared rays. They have longer wavelengths than visible light and are mostly produced by objects that give off heat, such as planets. With a process called interferometry, the VLT combines infrared rays coming from space using two or more linked telescopes. Computers process this information to create images of exoplanets. The combined images from the linked telescopes are much clearer than images made by a single telescope.

While only forty-one exoplanets have been found through direct imaging, that number may change in the near future. New technology and bigger and better telescopes may help scientists see much clearer images of the worlds beyond our solar system.

3 THE CLEAR COSMOS

Earth's atmosphere distorts light traveling from distant stars. To get clear views of celestial objects, space telescopes such as the Hubble (*above*) orbit above the atmosphere.

Twinkling stars—millions of flickering lights in the dark night—are beautiful and familiar, but have you ever wondered what causes that twinkling? It's something that is critical to our survival—Earth's atmosphere. This multilayered blanket of gases, particles, and liquids makes life on Earth possible. It traps heat and oxygen, a life-supporting gas. It guards us from the sun's harmful radiation and from incoming meteors (rocky or metallic objects that fly through space). But the atmosphere also distorts starlight. That's why stars appear to twinkle in space.

This twinkle is a problem in astronomy. It means the atmosphere is bending a star's light as it travels down to our eyes. This distortion makes a star's light—and its orbiting planets—difficult to study from Earth's surface, since many light waves are either blocked, blurred, or bent.

SEEING THE STARLIGHT

When astronomers observe a star's light through a telescope, the light often bounces around the circular area visible through the telescope. Astronomers call this circle the seeing disk. When astronomers speak of "poor seeing," they mean that the light bounces a lot. "Good seeing" means that a star's image is steady. Poor seeing is bad news for exoplanet research, since it most affects observations of planets and moons.

Several conditions affect how well astronomers see planets and stars from Earth. Our atmosphere is turbulent, filled with constantly moving gases, water droplets, and particles of dust and pollutants. Jet streams, or high-speed currents of warm and cold air, travel up to 50,000 feet (15,240 meters) above Earth's surface. These currents can carry ice or large clouds and rapidly move particles suspended in the air. This material is part of what blurs starlight traveling through the atmosphere. Light pollution also affects how well astronomers can see starlight. Light from buildings and streetlamps provides a steady glow in populated areas. The moon's light (reflected from the sun) also illuminates our night sky. This light diffuses, or thins, incoming starlight, making it appear dimmer than it actually is. Just look up at night in a city. You won't spot many stars. But far from a city, you'll see a much different night sky—one that is filled with brilliant stars and clouded by the Milky Way.

Avoiding light-diffusing factors is critical to astronomers. That's why the biggest and best telescopes on Earth are in isolated, dry, cold, and high-altitude areas. The air in these places has little moisture and few city lights to diffuse incoming starlight. And at high altitudes, the air contains less water vapor and other gases that blur starlight. One of the best areas for telescopes is Chile in South America. Universities, space agencies, and other groups from around the globe have built their biggest telescopes in this mountainous and arid country, which has few big cities and little light pollution.

GIANT EYES

Telescopes that detect visible light are called optical telescopes. They gather a large field of light and focus it to produce a magnified image of distant objects. The largest optical telescopes are called reflecting telescopes. They use mirrors to gather light. In a reflecting telescope, incoming light hits a large curved primary mirror, bounces off it onto a smaller secondary mirror, and travels to an eyepiece, where the user sees a crisp, bright, and clean image. Reflecting telescopes can operate only at night, since they collect light that would be overpowered by the sun's light during the day.

The Gemini South Observatory in Chile, high in the Andes Mountains and far from any big cities, offers astronomers superb views of the stars.

With reflecting telescopes, bigger mirrors are definitely better. Peering through the 60-mile-thick (97 km) atmosphere, Earth's largest reflecting telescopes see far into space. They are usually perched high up in the thinning atmosphere, where the view is much clearer.

But Earth's atmosphere causes interference for even the highest reflecting telescopes. To correct this interference, scientists use a system called adaptive optics. First, they use computers to measure the distortion of light caused by the atmosphere. They then make changes to the shape of a telescope's primary mirror to create a clearer image—basically erasing the twinkle. This process allows ground-based telescopes to produce images of stars that are almost as clear as those made by space telescopes.

Take the Keck Observatory, for example. Its twin telescopes sit atop dormant volcano Mauna Kea in Hawaii. At 14,000 feet (4,200 m) on the

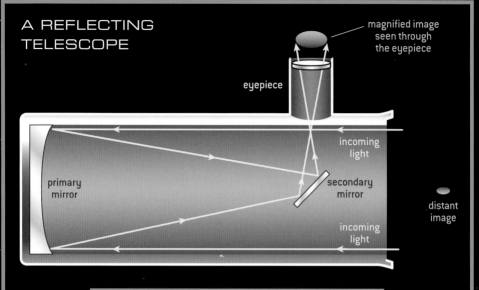

A REFLECTING TELESCOPE

magnified image seen through the eyepiece

eyepiece

incoming light

primary mirror

secondary mirror

incoming light

distant image

Inside a reflecting telescope, incoming light hits a primary mirror, bounces to a secondary mirror, and travels to an eyepiece, which magnifies the image. The larger the primary mirror, the more light it can collect—so it can collect faint light from distant stars.

mountain's ash- and snow-covered summit, the Keck telescopes are above the clouds. Little light pollution muddies the telescopes' views. The atmosphere is just about always clear above their primary mirrors, which measure 33 feet (10 m) across. Each mirror is made from thirty-six hexagonal (six-sided) segments. Using adaptive optics, engineers constantly adjust the segments to compensate for distortion caused by the atmosphere. The mirrors change shape two thousand times each second.

Keck has had many exoplanetary and space firsts. It recorded the first planetary transit seen by scientists, when Osiris traveled past its star, creating a shadow. In 2008 researchers at Keck identified water in two disks of material that were in the process of becoming planets. This was an incredible find, since planets that contain water might be able to support life. And in July 2015, Keck spotted the first Earthlike planet traveling around a sunlike star. The planet was Kepler-452b, first seen by the Kepler Space Telescope.

The largest optical telescope on land is in the Canary Islands, Spanish islands off the coast of West Africa in the Atlantic Ocean. The Gran Telescopio Canarias has a primary mirror measuring a whopping 34 feet (10 m) across. US astronomers have pioneered a new exoplanet observation method there. They use the Ohio State InfraRed Imager/Spectrometer (OSIRIS) to precisely measure light and to minimize atmospheric distortion.

TUNING INTO SPACE

If optical telescopes are Earth's eyes, radio telescopes are its ears. Day and night, their huge dishes and antennae receive radio waves from stars, planets, and quasars (starlike objects at the center of distant galaxies). Since radio waves from space are very weak, receiver dishes have to be big. They collect radio waves and focus them toward a suspended antenna. The antenna turns the waves into electric signals, which can then be analyzed by a computer. The atmosphere does little to interfere with incoming radio waves, but human-made radio interference is a problem. So radio telescopes are built in remote areas, far from most human radio transmissions. These telescopes can measure not only radio waves but also heat radiating from planets. Using spectrometers, radio telescopes can also detect 150 different kinds of molecules in space, including compounds such as water and carbon dioxide.

The largest radio telescope in the world is at the Arecibo Observatory in Puerto Rico, a US island commonwealth in the Caribbean Sea. Its receiver is 1,000 feet (305 m) across. This is the observatory where Aleksander Wolszczan and Dale Frail found three exoplanets in the early 1990s.

Arrays, or groupings, of small radio telescopes can take highly sensitive measurements of radio waves. The most sensitive radio telescope is the Very Large Array in central New Mexico. It contains twenty-seven dish antennae, each 82 feet (25 m) across. The array has gathered images of new planets forming around young stars.

This view of the Arecibo Observatory in Puerto Rico shows its massive dish receiver, which collects radio waves and sends them to the antenna suspended above it.

Built especially for exoplanet hunting by an international partnership is the Atacama Large Millimeter/submillimeter Array (ALMA) in Chile. At an elevation of 16,500 feet (5,030 m), the desert observatory uses sixty-six dish antennae, with a total collecting area of 71,000 square feet (6,600 sq. m). Scientists use ALMA to view the early stages of planetary formation and to map the gas and dust (the building blocks of new exoplanets and solar systems) of the Milky Way and other galaxies. In late 2015, a team of astronomers using ALMA found gas giants orbiting four young stars.

FLYING OBSERVATORIES

Getting above most of Earth's atmosphere is another way to avoid its distortion. To do this, scientists use different kinds of aircraft. Sounding rockets have scientific instruments attached to their nose cones. After being launched, the rockets soar into and then above the atmosphere for five to twenty minutes. The instruments record X-ray data coming from space and then fall back to Earth. Scientists pick them up and study the recorded data. Astronomers also use high-altitude, unpiloted helium-filled balloons to carry scientific instruments and telescopes 22 miles (35 km) above the ground. At this height, the balloons float above 99.7 percent of Earth's atmosphere, where they measure X-rays and gamma rays from space.

The most advanced and largest flying observatory is a modified Boeing 747 jet aircraft called the Stratospheric Observatory for Infrared Astronomy (SOFIA). It holds a telescope with an 8.2-foot-wide (2.5 m) mirror that can detect infrared radiation. The jet carries the telescope to an altitude of 41,000 feet (12,500 m) above Earth, where it measures infrared radiation from planets, stars, and galaxies. SOFIA's other instruments include cameras, spectrometers, and photometers (to measure luminosity). In 2013 scientists used SOFIA to view the transit of HD 189733b. This hot Jupiter orbits its star every 2.2 days. It was the first exoplanet spotted with SOFIA.

SPACE TELESCOPES

SOFIA and other flying observatories offer a clearer view for astronomers, but the clearest view can only be found past Earth's atmosphere—in space. The incredibly clear images captured by space telescopes have made more of space and its objects accessible to people on Earth. The first space telescopes were not designed to find exoplanets, but they have found some anyway. Some later space telescopes were designed just for finding exoplanets and have had amazing results. Their images have shown us not only exoplanets but also nebulae, solar systems, galaxies, and other objects in the universe.

A telescope up in Earth's orbit has many advantages. It works twenty-four hours a day and is not limited to only nighttime observations like ground-based optical telescopes. Weather cannot limit its view, and the atmosphere has no blurring effects either. Orbiting telescopes give astronomers and astrophysicists exactly what they crave—priceless information about and breathtaking images of the cosmos.

THE VIEW FROM HUBBLE

Romanian rocketry pioneer Hermann Oberth first proposed sending a large telescope into space in 1923. US astrophysicist Lyman Spitzer proposed the idea again in 1946. On April 24, 1990, Spitzer's proposal became a reality when the Hubble Space Telescope was launched into Earth's orbit aboard the US space shuttle *Discovery*. Costing about $2.5 billion to build, this bus-sized telescope was the first major space observatory. Its images would become iconic, showing us alien landscapes we could previously only imagine.

Immediately after launch, the Hubble suffered serious operational problems. Astronauts traveled in space shuttles to fix the Hubble five times. This work involved arduous space walks (any work astronauts do outside a spacecraft). Despite needing repairs, the telescope has advanced our knowledge of the universe. With its relatively narrow (7.9 feet, or 2.4 m across) primary mirror, the telescope has made 1.2 million astronomical observations in the infrared, ultraviolet, and visible waves of the spectrum.

Some of its biggest discoveries include determining that the universe is about 13.7 billion years old and that black holes reside at the centers of galaxies. The telescope has also captured breathtaking images, such as *The Pillars of Creation*, a picture of the Eagle Nebula, in our galaxy. The image shows richly colored pillar-like clouds of interstellar gas and dust.

Hubble has also helped us understand exoplanets and solar system formation. In 2001 scientists used Hubble to determine the makeup of an atmosphere of an exoplanet 150 light-years away. The telescope took the first direct image of an exoplanet in 2008. The planet is three times the size of Jupiter, orbiting the Fomalhaut star in a solar system 25 light-years from Earth. Hubble also discovered a previously unknown type of exoplanet—a water world (a planet with a globe-covering ocean) with a thick and steamy atmosphere.

Scientists are bound to find many more exoplanets within Hubble's abundant data. It's just a matter of searching through the information it gathers. But while Hubble continues to function, its life is ending. In 2011 the US space shuttle program ended. So it is impossible for astronauts to service the telescope again. Hubble is expected to continue working into at least 2018.

HUBBLE'S GLASSES ....

Getting Hubble to its launch and its first clear images was an incredibly difficult journey. A project of that magnitude had never been attempted before. Scientists anxiously awaited the first images to return to Earth after the telescope's systems went live. After a few weeks, the images came in—but something was seriously wrong. Instead of clear images of stars, Hubble's images were blurry. After many tests, NASA scientists determined that the telescope's main mirror was slightly flawed—it was a tiny bit too flat at its edges, by a measurement equal to one-fiftieth the width of a human hair. The mirror's manufacturer had used a faulty device to test the shape of the mirror. The error was a public relations disaster for NASA: its biggest project, which had cost an exorbitant amount of taxpayer money, could take only blurry pictures.

Soon scientists were working on a fix for the flawed mirror. They developed Corrective Optics Space Telescope Axial Replacement (COSTAR), a device made from five thousand parts that basically functioned as eyeglasses for the telescope. Astronauts trained for thousands of hours to perform the difficult and dangerous task of installing COSTAR in space. In late 1993, NASA sent up Hubble's first servicing mission. Five tense days after the space shuttle returned to Earth, the first images came back from the repaired Hubble. Edward Weiler, the chief scientist for the Hubble program, recalled the moment when the images came in: "About 50 astronomers and institute engineers were gathered around a screen and that first picture came down. And that is the moment I knew we had fixed it. The first image had a star right in the center. It was only that star, but it was crystal sharp clear. . . . People just went crazy."

To NASA's relief, COSTAR had worked. Soon Hubble was living up to its hype and sending back the clearest images yet seen of the cosmos.

The Hubble Space Telescope captured this dramatic picture of the Eagle Nebula in 1995. NASA scientists named the image *The Pillars of Creation* because stars are being created inside the nebula.

CLEARER AND CLEARER VIEWS

While Hubble may be the superstar of space telescopes, it certainly is not alone in Earth's orbit. Many other orbiting telescopes have searched the skies for exoplanets, and more are on their way.

In 1999, nine years after Hubble was launched, the Chandra X-ray Observatory took its place in Earth's orbit. This telescope, named after

Indian American astrophysicist Subrahmanyan Chandrasekhar, is located in an elliptical (oval) orbit that is two hundred times higher above Earth than the Hubble Space Telescope. Like optical telescopes, X-ray telescopes contain mirrors, but they are configured differently. X-ray energy travels much faster than visible light. It would pierce through and be absorbed by a single mirror. So Chandra carries four pairs of mirrors arranged in a barrel shape. This shape allows X-ray energy to bounce from one mirror to another without damaging them, enabling the telescope to capture information carried by the X-rays.

Chandra tracks X-rays traveling from black holes, stars that are forming, and stars that are exploding. In 2013 Chandra detected an

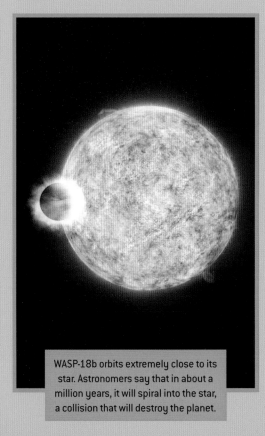

WASP-18b orbits extremely close to its star. Astronomers say that in about a million years, it will spiral into the star, a collision that will destroy the planet.

exoplanet transiting its star. It was an exciting moment—the first time X-rays had revealed an exoplanet. The X-rays showed the planet, called HD 189733b, to be a close-orbiting hot Jupiter with an atmosphere. In 2014 Chandra found WASP-18b, a planet ten times the size of Jupiter and 330 light-years from Earth. Ignazio Pillitteri of the National Institute for Astrophysics in Palermo, Italy, said, "WASP-18b is an extreme exoplanet . . . one of the most massive hot Jupiters known and one of the closest to its host star."

Also important to exoplanet research is NASA's Spitzer Space Telescope, which sees energy from the infrared side of the electromagnetic spectrum. Launched in 2003, the Spitzer measures infrared light coming from exoplanets and analyzes that light to measure the temperature, winds, and atmospheric makeup of exoplanets.

Spitzer, which was designed to find objects hidden in interstellar dust, has proven to be essential in determining the characteristics of exoplanets. Spitzer's data identified the first exoplanet found to have water. In 2007 it found a planet with surface winds traveling up to 6,000 miles (9,660 km) per hour. It found another planet, Upsilon Andromedae b, with temperatures that vary an incredible 2,550°F (1,417°C) from day to night. It found a hot Jupiter that is missing the gas methane, which goes against all that scientists previously knew about hot Jupiters. In 2014 scientists used data from Spitzer and Hubble to examine the atmospheres of ten exoplanets. They were looking for water, and they found that some of the exoplanets had much cloudier atmospheres than others. The presence of clouds shows that the planets likely have water on their surfaces.

While Spitzer wasn't designed for exoplanet research, a mission called Convection, Rotation, and Planetary Transits (CoRoT) was. This ESA telescope, launched in 2006, was designed in part to use the transit detection method to find rocky exoplanets that orbit close to their stars. The telescope was small, with just an 11-inch (27 cm) mirror, but it made some important exoplanet discoveries. CoRoT found its first exoplanet in 2007. In 2009 CoRoT found the smallest rocky exoplanet yet discovered—one just twice the size of Earth. After more than six years in space, CoRoT's systems failed. Its mission officially ended in June 2013.

KEPLER: THE EXOPLANET MOTHER LODE

As exoplanet discoveries started gaining momentum, NASA developed a space telescope with the sole mission of finding Earthlike exoplanets. The Kepler Space Telescope launched in 2009 and immediately began finding transiting exoplanets with its 37-inch (94 cm) telescope. For the first part of its mission, Kepler continuously observed 150,000 stars in the Cygnus and Lyra constellations. After its launch, this telescope hit the mother lode of exoplanet detection, finding more than four thousand possible exoplanets in 2,258 days. Scientists confirmed that more than one thousand objects in that group are exoplanets.

A rocket carrying the Kepler Space Telescope blasts into the sky in March 2009. A sign on the craft states its mission to "search for Earth-size planets."

In May 2016, NASA scientists announced that within Kepler's data were another 1,284 confirmed exoplanets. More than five hundred of them are believed to be rocky planets and possibly in habitable orbits around their stars. Kepler's findings have changed how scientists view the cosmos. According to NASA's Paul Hertz, "Before the Kepler space telescope launched, we did not know whether exoplanets were rare or common in the galaxy. Thanks to Kepler and the research community, we now know there could be more planets than stars."

Kepler was designed to last just one year in space—but it went on to operate for four years. In 2013 a mechanical failure stopped Kepler from

The Kepler Space Telescope found Kepler-452b (*right*) in July 2015. A super-Earth, the planet travels in the Goldilocks zone around its star.

being able to direct its telescope toward specific star fields. Some thought the failure meant the end of Kepler. John Troeltzsch, the Kepler mission program manager, felt "sorrow, disappointment, a little grief in there." But instead of scrapping the telescope, engineer Doug Wiemer of Ball Aerospace (the company that built the telescope) came up with a new plan. He thought of the one thing the crippled telescope could lean on: sunlight. He figured out how to use sunlight's bombarding photons (particles that make up light) to push against the spacecraft and keep it in a stable orbit.

Wiemer's idea led to a redesign of Kepler's mission, and in 2014, Kepler 2 (K2) was born. The redesigned telescope can view only a ribbon of sky as it orbits the sun, but it's still finding exoplanets. From 2014 to 2015, K2 found more than one hundred confirmed exoplanets. One of its discoveries was a system of three super-Earths orbiting the same star, and one of these planets is in the Goldilocks zone and could possibly contain liquid water. "The outermost planet is kind of like Earth or Venus in terms of how hot it would be, the second is more like Mercury, and the innermost planet is hotter still," said Ian Crossfield, an astronomer at the University of Arizona in Tucson. It was one of many exciting finds for scientists, who hope that the K2 mission and other space telescopes will continue to reveal exoplanets.

4 STRANGE WORLDS

After learning what a planet is made of and how far it sits from its sun, astronomers can make guesses about its surface. This illustration shows an imagined view of one of three planets orbiting 2MASS J23062928-0502285, a dwarf star 40 light-years from Earth.

It's very exciting. You realise that our solar system is just one example of the many ways that nature is building planets.

—*Didier Queloz, astronomer, 2005*

As space and ground telescopes keep hauling in their exoplanet bounties, scientists are more and more amazed by what is being found. Some exoplanets are so different and strange that they are redefining previous planet formation theories. Telescopes have discovered super-gigantic planets, planets with oddly eccentric orbits, and more. Their existence challenges all that we know about how solar systems form and the types of planets that can orbit within them. For centuries scientists had only our solar system to study. They assumed that all systems were like ours. With exoplanet research, scientists can see that maybe no two systems are alike—and each one may be filled with unique surprises.

Scientists have more than three thousand confirmed exoplanets to study and close to five thousand exoplanet candidates that have not yet been confirmed. The closest possibly habitable exoplanet—located in its solar system's Goldilocks zone—is Wolf-1061, found in late 2015. It is 14 light-years away from Earth. Even in a spacecraft flying at 36,000 miles (58,000 km) per hour, it would take more than 250,000 years to reach this planet. While we can't visit an exoplanet anytime soon, we can explore the data scientists have collected on exoplanets to see what kinds of worlds are in the universe.

HOME OF THE ANCIENT EARTHS

The solar system Kepler-444 is known as the Home of the Ancient Earths. This system—five rocky, Earth-sized planets orbiting a sunlike star—is the oldest known solar system of its kind in our galaxy. Kepler-444, near the constellation Lyra in the Milky Way, formed 11.2 billion years ago. That makes it almost as old as the universe itself, which formed about 13.7 billion years ago, and about two and half times older than Earth. Kepler-444's star formed before most other stars in the galaxy. All the tightly packed planets in the system orbit the star in less than ten days. The Home of the Ancient Earths was discovered on January 27, 2015, by the Kepler Space Telescope.

According to astronomer Tiago Campante, from the University of Birmingham in the United Kingdom, "By the time the Earth formed, the planets in this system were already older than our planet is today. This discovery may now help to pinpoint the beginning of what we might call the 'era of planet formation.'" This is the time shortly after the beginning of the universe when planets began forming.

THE BIG ORBITER

The planet 2MASS J2126 (also known as the Big Orbiter) was once thought to be a lonely rogue planet, unattached to any star. Scientists then determined that the Big Orbiter does have a star—it's just extremely far away. The planet travels at a distance of 620 billion miles (1 trillion km) from its star. That is seven thousand times Earth's distance from the sun. Scientists believe it takes 2MASS J2126 about nine hundred thousand years to complete one orbit. That's the largest orbit around its star in the Milky Way.

This giant planet, discovered on January 22, 2016, is 11.6 to 15 times the mass of Jupiter. It has a scorching hot surface temperature of 2,730°F (1,500°C).

Niall Deacon of the University of Hertfordshire in the United Kingdom remarked, "This is the widest planet system found so far, and both [its star

THE DISAPPEARING PLANET · · · · · · · · · · · · · ·

In 2012 scientists believed they had found a planet in the nearest star system to Earth—just 4.3 light-years away. Xavier Dumusque of the Harvard-Smithsonian Center for Astrophysics had searched through data and believed he had found a wobble in the path of the system's star, Alpha Centauri. The wobble was small though, so Dumusque thought a small planet, named Alpha Centauri Bb, not a gas giant, was causing it.

But Vinesh Rajpaul, a graduate student in astrophysics at the University of Oxford in the United Kingdom, suspected that Dumusque was incorrect. Rajpaul created a computer simulation that showed how other factors, such as sunspots (dark, cool areas) on a star's surface, equipment problems, or the gravitational pull of another star, could create the appearance of a wobble. With new analysis in 2015, the team showed that Alpha Centauri Bb was just a phantom, created by unclear data. Even Dumusque and his team agreed, saying, "We are not 100 percent sure, but probably the planet is not there."

and planet] have been known for eight years. But nobody had made the link between the objects before. The planet is not quite as lonely as we first thought, but it's certainly in a very long-distance relationship."

THE REAL HOTH

OGLE-2005-BLG-390 is an icy and rocky planet nicknamed Hoth, after an icy planet featured in the *Star Wars* movies. This super-Earth is five times the size of Earth. It was discovered on January 26, 2006, by microlensing.

This real-life Hoth takes eight years and 363 days to orbit its star. It is 21,527 light-years from Earth. This small icy planet is the first of its size found orbiting a sunlike star. Its chilly surface temperature is likely about −364°F (−220°C). According to Andrew Williams, an astronomer at the Perth Observatory in Australia, "The only substances able to form a planet of that size, at that temperature, are rock and ice. And during formation, the rock, being heavier, would have sunk to the middle. Pluto and many of Saturn's and Jupiter's moons are similar."

EARTH'S TWIN?

Kepler-22b orbits 620 light-years from Earth. This planet with continents of land is 2.4 times the size of Earth and may be water-covered. It was discovered in December 2011 by the transit method. It takes 290 days to orbit its star, a few months less than Earth's 365-day orbit.

This planet orbits within the habitable zone of its sunlike star. Its surface temperature is about 72°F (22°C), which is the right temperature for liquid water, and liquid water is a marker for possible life. Alan Boss, from the Carnegie Institution for Science in Washington, DC, who helped identify the planet, says, "This discovery supports the growing belief that we live in a universe crowded with life."

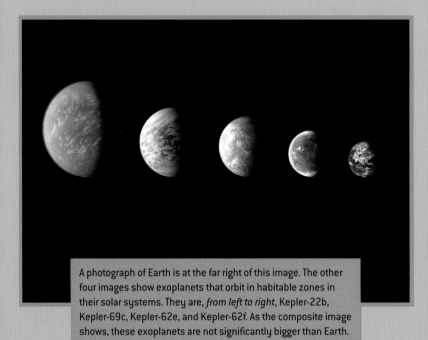

A photograph of Earth is at the far right of this image. The other four images show exoplanets that orbit in habitable zones in their solar systems. They are, *from left to right*, Kepler-22b, Kepler-69c, Kepler-62e, and Kepler-62f. As the composite image shows, these exoplanets are not significantly bigger than Earth.

THE SUNSCREEN PLANET

The hot Jupiter WASP-33b orbits 379 light-years from Earth. Scientists have detected that this hot and large exoplanet has a lower atmosphere and an upper atmosphere, or stratosphere. It was discovered in June 2015 by the transit method using the Hubble Space Telescope.

Scientists believe that the temperature reaches 3,000°F (1,650°C) in the planet's lower atmosphere and 6,000°F (3,315°C) in its stratosphere. Avi Mandell, a planetary scientist at NASA's Goddard Space Flight Center in Maryland, said of this kind of planet, "Some of these planets are so hot in their upper atmospheres, they're essentially boiling off into space."

What's strange about this planet is that the stratosphere acts as a kind of sunscreen layer around the planet. Scientists have detected titanium oxide in the stratosphere. This chemical, which is often used as an ingredient in sunscreen, absorbs visible and ultraviolet radiation. The planet also orbits its star clockwise, the opposite direction of most exoplanets.

THE ZOMBIE PLANET

Just 25 light-years from Earth is Fomalhaut b, a planet that orbits its star through a vast minefield of debris and dust. Scientists found Fomalhaut b in 2008 through direct imaging using the Hubble Space Telescope. At first they thought it was just a dust cloud. Then, in 2012, new analysis revealed it to be a planet. In a way, this discovery brought the planet back from the dead, so scientists nicknamed it the Zombie Planet.

Fomalhaut b is three times the size of Jupiter and has a very long orbit of 872 years. It travels through a giant debris belt (14 billion to 20 billion miles, or 22.5 billion to 32.1 billion km, wide) that stretches around its parent star. Fomalhaut b has an elliptical orbit. When it is closest to its star, it is 10.7 billion miles (17.2 billion km) away. When farthest, it is 27 billion miles (43.4 billion km) away.

TrES-4 is a planet of extremes. It is extremely large, extremely lightweight, and extremely hot. It also has an extremely short orbit—just four days.

Paul Kalas is a researcher with the University of California—Berkeley and the SETI (Search for Extraterrestrial Intelligence) Institute, a private research organization formed to seek out life in the universe. He says of the planet, "We are shocked [by the extreme orbit of this planet]. This is not what we expected."

THE CORK PLANET

Scientists have also discovered a very strange planet 1,605 light-years from Earth. TrES-4 is one of the largest exoplanets ever found. It is also one of the lightest. This hot Jupiter was discovered in 2007 by the transit method. Its orbit is a short four days.

While very large, TrES-4 is only about as dense as cork. If it were put into a giant pool of water, this exoplanet would float. It is also a very hot planet, with scorching surface temperatures about 2,300°F (1,260°C).

The denser an object in space, the greater its gravitation pull. Because TrES-4's density is so low, its gravity is very weak. In fact, rather than being held around the planet by gravity, some of its atmosphere is escaping into space. Scientist Georgi Mandushev from the Lowell Observatory in Arizona says, "TrES-4 is the largest known exoplanet. Because of the planet's relatively weak pull on its upper atmosphere, some of the atmosphere probably escapes in a comet-like tail."

THE OOZER

A super-Earth called 55 Cancri e orbits its star 41 light-years from Earth. Discovered in 2004 by radial velocity, this rocky planet has an eighteen-hour orbit that brings it very close to its parent star. It is tidally locked to that star (one side of the planet always faces the star). It's always daytime on that side of the planet and always nighttime on the other side.

The super-Earth 55 Cancri e orbits extremely close to its star. It's so hot that it oozes lavalike fluids.

This planet is hot, reaching 4,400°F (2,427°C) on the day side and 2,060°F (1,127°C) on the night side. It also contains fluids that at such high temperatures ooze like lava from its rocks.

According to Nikku Madhusudhan, a researcher at Yale University in Connecticut, "The surface of this planet is likely covered in graphite and diamond rather than water and granite. . . . This is our first glimpse of a rocky world with a fundamentally different chemistry from Earth."

THE CRAZY ORBITER

Traveling 190 light-years away from Earth, is HD 80606b. This strange planet has a very odd orbit and extreme temperatures. It shows signs of extreme weather as well. This hot Jupiter was discovered in 2001 by radial velocity.

This planet swings out to almost the distance Earth is from the sun during its 111-day orbit. Then, for less than a day, it gets very close to its star—closer than Mercury is to the sun.

Greg Laughlin of the Lick Observatory in California says that "if you could float above the clouds of this planet" as it zooms toward its star on its odd orbit, "you'd see its sun growing larger and larger at faster and faster rates, increasing in brightness by almost a factor of 1,000." As the planet nears the star, it heats up quickly. Within six hours, its temperature soars from 980°F to 2,240°F (527°C to 1,227°C).

THE REAL TATOOINE

Just like the planet Tatooine from the *Star Wars* films, Kepler-16b is a circumbinary planet. It orbits twin stars, so it has double sunrises and sunsets. This planet is the size of Saturn but is 50 percent denser. Kepler-16b is very cold and made of gas. The Kepler Space Telescope discovered it on September 15, 2011. It has a 229-day orbit and is 200 light-years from Earth. It was the first circumbinary planet ever found.

Before finding Kepler-16b, scientists thought that planets did not exist around twin stars. The discovery of Kepler-16b proved that this wasn't true.

PLANET NINE?

Even our own solar system has secrets. The system has eight planets plus the dwarf planet Pluto. But scientists may have discovered a mysterious "Planet Nine" orbiting at the outer limits of the solar system. In January 2016, planetary scientists Konstantin Batygin and Mike Brown at the California Institute of Technology announced evidence of a Neptune-sized planet in an average fifteen-thousand-year elliptical orbit of the sun. If it exists, the planet's average orbit would be about twenty times farther from the sun than Neptune's orbit.

Batygin and Brown studied six objects with unusual orbits in the Kuiper Belt, a band of icy and rocky objects orbiting beyond Neptune. The scientists believe that a ninth planet's gravitational pull has carried these objects into their strange orbits. While they have not seen the planet directly, Batygin and Brown have used mathematics and computer modeling to make their hypothesis. Of the find, Brown said, "There have only been two true planets discovered since ancient times, and this would be a third. It's a pretty substantial chunk of our solar system that's still out there to be found, which is pretty exciting."

An imagined view of Planet Nine, with the Milky Way stretching behind it and our sun off to the right. The orbit of Neptune is shown as a faint ring around the sun.

This image shows Kepler-16b (*center*), with the two stars it orbits in the background. On a planet that orbits two stars, sunrises and sunsets occur twice a day.

Although this planet is probably too cold and gaseous to hold life, other circumbinary planets might be habitable. That's because having two stars at the center of a solar system instead of just one extends the system's Goldilocks zone, creating a larger area where conditions for life are favorable. According to NASA's William Borucki, "Opportunities for life are much broader [if planets orbit two stars] than if planets form only around single stars."

THE PINK PLANET

The gas giant GJ 504b orbits 57 light-years from Earth. This young planet still glows with heat from its formation in a solar system that is 160 million years old. Compared with our solar system, which is 4.5 billion years old, this system is pretty young.

Discovered in 2013 by direct imaging, this planet orbits its star every 259 years and sixty-three days. This planet glows in shades of pink, purple,

GJ 504b glows magenta because it is still cooling down from its formation 160 million years ago.

and red, with its surface temperature reaching 460°F (237°C). Michael McElwain, a member of the discovery team at NASA's Goddard Space Flight Center, notes, "If we could travel to this giant planet, we would see a world still glowing from the heat of its formation with a color reminiscent of a dark cherry blossom, a dull magenta."

5

EARTH 2.0

Millions of plant and animal species live on Earth. Has life developed on other planets?

We are alive. We are intelligent. We must know.

—Stephen Hawking, physicist, on the search for life beyond Earth, 2015

When seen from space and when the sun's light hits it right, Earth glows blue—revealing its life-sustaining abundance of liquid water. In February 1990, the spacecraft *Voyager 1*, which had been launched in 1977, took its last images of Earth as it left our solar system. At a distance of 4 billion miles (6 billion km), Earth looked like a tiny pale blue dot in the vast blackness of space. Considering that image, US astronomer Carl Sagan wrote, "Our planet is a lonely speck in the great enveloping cosmic dark. . . . The Earth is the only world known so far to harbor life. There is nowhere else, at least in the near future, to which our species could migrate."

When Sagan wrote these words in 1997, the first few exoplanets had just been confirmed. A few decades later, known exoplanets were in the thousands. Among the multitude of planets found (and those yet to be discovered), is it possible that another pale blue dot exists? Many scientists believe so and are on the hunt for Earth 2.0—and the possibility of life elsewhere in our universe.

LOOKING FOR GOLDILOCKS

Where might life appear? We have only one way to determine this—by studying the only place where life is known to exist: Earth.

GREETINGS FROM PLANET EARTH · · · · · · · · ·

In 1977 the spacecraft *Voyager 1* and *Voyager 2* launched from Earth. They began their journey to the outermost regions of our solar system and were designed to observe Jupiter and Saturn as they flew by. *Voyager 2* also flew by Neptune and Uranus. Both spacecraft continued beyond the solar system. In 2012 *Voyager 1* left the solar system and entered interstellar space—the space between stars. This is the farthest that a human-made spacecraft has yet traveled, and *Voyager 1* continues hurtling forward in space. *Voyager 2* is headed to interstellar space as well and has reached the heliosphere, the outer layer of the solar system.

Voyager 1 and *Voyager 2* would be especially interesting to any intelligent life that might find the spacecraft. They each contain a gold record encoded with both sounds and images. The sounds include music, ranging from Johann Sebastian Bach's classical composition Brandenburg Concerto No. 2 to Chuck Berry's early rock song "Johnny B. Goode." Greetings in fifty-four human languages speak of peace and good wishes to unknown beings. Another greeting is the song of humpback whales. Other sounds include erupting volcanoes, Morse code signals, and a human baby crying. The records also hold photographs of scenes from Earth, ranging from a Guatemalan man to a street scene in Asia and an astronaut in space. The golden records were included on the two spacecraft with the hope that intelligent life may find them and understand something of us—a first connection between humans and other life in the universe.

Scientists have looked at Earth's position in our solar system and at Earth's temperature. Earth travels in our solar system's Goldilocks zone. In this zone, a planet's surface temperature stays between 32°F and 212°F (0°C and 100°C). This is the temperature at which water takes the form of liquid, and many scientists agree that liquid water is the key component for the appearance of life. In addition to being in the Goldilocks zone, a planet must have enough mass—and enough gravity—to sustain an atmosphere. An atmosphere protects life from dangerous radiation from stars and also traps the heat and gases needed for life to exist. If a planet is too small, it will not have enough gravitational pull to hold an atmosphere around its surface.

In our solar system, the habitable zone stretches from a little less than 93 million miles (150 million km) to 186 million miles (300 million km) from the sun, and Earth sits at 93 million miles. This zone is different in every solar system though. It all depends on the size and behavior of the star. A star that is larger than the sun emits more light and energy. Being too close to that energy would make for a harsher and hotter planetary environment, unsuitable for life. That would mean the Goldilocks zone would

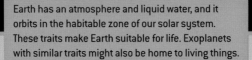

Earth has an atmosphere and liquid water, and it orbits in the habitable zone of our solar system. These traits make Earth suitable for life. Exoplanets with similar traits might also be home to living things.

need to be farther away from the star. If the star were smaller, planets in the Goldilocks zone would orbit much closer to the star. But smaller stars have a tendency to flare. Flares are sudden bursts of energy from a star's surface. This energy can tear away a planet's atmosphere. So planets orbiting close to small stars might not be habitable.

PLANETARY GUARDIANS

It's not just the atmosphere and the planet's distance from its star that are important for habitability. It also matters what other objects are in the solar system. For instance, the gravity of a moon orbiting a planet stabilizes it—keeping the planet in the same position as it orbits its star. In 1993 two French physicists, Jacques Laskar and Philippe Robutel, calculated that without the moon, Earth's tilt might be radically different. Instead of its 23-degree tilt in relation to the sun, Earth might tilt more extremely. That tilt might frequently change, with 90-degree swings. Life could not exist with the radical temperature changes caused by such a tilt. Without the moon, therefore, life may never have evolved on Earth.

If you look at pictures of the moon, you'll see that it is dented with huge craters. They resulted from a downpour of meteorites in the early history of the solar system. The meteorite showers also hit Earth. Scientists estimate that the showers ended 4 billion years ago and that life on Earth began about 3.9 billion years ago—just 100 million years after the last meteorites hit. If those meteorite showers had not ended when they did, life may not have had a chance to develop. Rock and dust from the meteorites would have filled the air and blocked sunlight from reaching the planet's surface, killing any plants and other life that might have been forming.

According to planetary formation theorist George Wetherill of the Carnegie Institution in Washington, DC, Jupiter might also have played a role in the development of life on Earth. Jupiter, the most massive planet in our solar system, may have served as a shield for Earth, absorbing many meteorites before they could reach our planet.

FINDING LIFE

Even if a planet is in the Goldilocks zone and has water, an atmosphere, and other favorable conditions for life, there is still no guarantee that life will evolve on its surface. No one is sure how life began on Earth, although scientists have different theories. One is the primordial soup concept—the idea that organic molecules, made of carbon atoms, mixed and chemically reacted in a pool of water to form the first living cell. Some scientists theorize that organic molecules came from space—landing on Earth inside a comet, an icy body traveling around the sun in a long elliptical orbit. Another theory describes the emergence of life near deep-sea vents, openings on an ocean floor that spew hot water mixed with minerals. There, deep underwater, meteorites would not have damaged developing life. And even if Earth's early atmosphere was thin, without enough oxygen or carbon dioxide to support life, organisms might still have developed on the seafloor. Maybe a combination of these scenarios happened.

Scientists don't know how life began on Earth. One theory says that organic molecules came to our planet inside a comet.

EXTREME LIFE ·····················

What might life be like on an exoplanet? To find out, astrobiologists study extremophiles—animals, bacteria, and plants that live in extreme environments on Earth. Extremophiles have been found living in places previously believed to be uninhabitable, such as extremely hot, cold, acidic, and salty environments. Astrobiologists say that if some living things can survive in extreme conditions on Earth, other kinds of life might be able to survive in extreme conditions on other planets.

Thermophiles are extremophiles that live in very hot places, such as near deep-sea vents, where temperatures can reach 750°F (400°C). At the depths of the vents, as far down as 3 miles (5 km) below the ocean's surface, no sunlight reaches the organisms and the water is filled with toxic minerals. But thermophile bacteria there survive by changing the toxic minerals into forms of energy.

Other extremophiles, called psychrophiles, thrive in extremely cold temperatures. These organisms are especially interesting to astrobiologists, who believe life may be found in very cold environments in space. One place where psychrophiles exist is in Organic Lake in eastern Antarctica. Its water temperatures often fall to 9°F (–13°C), but its high salt content keeps the water from freezing. The water is filled with psychrophilic life—from algae to bacteria and viruses.

Some creatures thrive in extremely salty water. In Mono Lake in California, some bacteria live in the salty water. Others live in the lake's mud, which lacks oxygen, and they survive by ingesting sulfur from the mud's minerals. Acidophiles can survive in very acidic environments, such as inside certain caves. In these caves, oxygen combines with hydrogen sulfide to make sulfuric acid. The bacteria that live there create a slime that protects them from the acid, which would kill most other living things.

Microscopic creatures called tardigrades are some of the hardiest animals on Earth. They can live in freezing temperatures, extreme heat, and extreme ocean depths. They can also withstand high levels of deadly radiation. In 2007 scientists put thousands of tardigrades on a satellite, which was launched into space. There the creatures lived in an environment without air pressure (the force of air pressing on things on Earth) and were exposed to deadly levels of radiation. Under such conditions, without protective space suits or spacecraft, humans would die in less than a minute. Some of the tardigrades did die in space. But others fared well. When the satellite returned to Earth, scientists found that many of the tardigrades were still alive. Some had even had babies.

Tardigrades and other extremophiles can survive in environments that are deadly to most other life-forms. So scientists think perhaps living things can survive in extreme conditions on other planets.

However life appeared, its existence is related to the makeup of our atmosphere. The US Galileo probe, launched in 1989, studied Earth's atmosphere on its way to Jupiter. It found three markers for life: chlorophyll (a substance produced by plants), oxygen (created in large amounts by plants), and methane (created by certain bacteria). Methane, when mixed with oxygen, forms water molecules and carbon dioxide. These three markers comprise Earth's biosignature, or evidence for life, and scientists can use it as a baseline to study exoplanetary atmospheres. If an exoplanet also contains these markers in its biosignature and if the planet is in the Goldilocks zone, life might possibly exist there.

Astrobiology is the study of life's origins on Earth and the search for it in the universe. In addition to studying life on Earth, astrobiologists look to other planets in our solar system to discover whether life once existed there. If scientists can find evidence of life on another planet in our solar system, even if it is long gone, it is highly likely that life has appeared in other solar systems.

Searching for evidence of life is one of the objectives of NASA's Mars Science Laboratory mission, which sent a rover named *Curiosity* to Mars in 2011. Mars also sits in our solar system's habitable zone and is the most Earthlike planet. It contains frozen water and an atmosphere, although the atmosphere is very thin and doesn't provide much protection from the sun's radiation. Since landing in 2012, the rover has been looking for evidence of microbes (microscopic life-forms) living on Mars. So far *Curiosity* has found that the planet has the right chemistry for life to exist. It has hydrogen, oxygen, phosphorus, and sulfur. The rover has also found carbon molecules, a building block for life. Methane also exists in Mars's atmosphere, and the rover has found evidence of an ancient stream. Some scientists think that oceans might have covered Mars in its past and that dark, salty water may still flow there. While no remains of life (as we know it) have yet been found, Mars certainly has life's raw ingredients. Perhaps *Curiosity* will find evidence of a new kind of life underground, one that is not easily recognizable by humans.

The NASA rover *Curiosity* has been searching for signs of life on Mars since 2012.

Two future NASA missions to search for evidence of life in the solar system are planned. One is set to study Jupiter's moon Europa and the other to study Saturn's moon Titan. While Europa is very cold, scientists believe liquid water exists beneath its icy crust. If deep-sea vents exist at the bottom of those bodies of water, the possibility for life in the water could be strong. An orbiting spacecraft, set to launch in the 2020s, will carry instruments that will be able to see through the ice and analyze whatever may be below. The Titan Saturn System Mission, with no set launch date, will explore seas found on Titan's surface. Scientists are very interested in exploring this moon, as it is the most Earthlike object in our solar system, with a thick atmosphere and organic molecules.

Life may be found very soon. Scientists know what to look for, and they are searching. NASA chief scientist Ellen Stofan agrees, saying in 2015, "I think we're going to have strong indications of life beyond Earth within a decade, and I think we're going to have definitive evidence within 20 to 30 years."

THE SEARCH FOR EXTRATERRESTRIAL INTELLIGENCE

Before the first exoplanet was even found, Frank Drake, a US radio astronomer, was searching for intelligent life beyond Earth. In 1961 Drake set out to determine how many intelligent civilizations might exist in the Milky Way. He estimated the number of stars in the galaxy, the number of stars that might have planets, the number of planets that could potentially support life, the number of planets on which life may have actually developed, the odds of that life being intelligent, the odds of that life being able to send communications into space, and other factors from which he created the Drake equation. According to this equation, the Milky Way could hold up to 140,000 intelligent civilizations.

In 1984 Drake founded the SETI Institute, formed to search for life beyond Earth. SETI scientists and researchers study astrobiology and try to detect intelligent life through radio and light signals that might have been deliberately sent by extraterrestrial beings. While SETI has not yet found evidence of life, the institute continues the search with several long-term research projects.

In 2016 astronomers Adam Frank of the University of Rochester in New York and Woodruff Sullivan at the University of Washington revisited Drake's equation. They calculated a far larger number of possible intelligent civilizations than Drake had: one trillion. To reach their conclusion, they considered civilizations that may have existed at some point during the entire fourteen-billion-year history of the universe.

THE STARSHADE PROJECT

To find the markers of life in an exoplanet's atmosphere, scientists must first find a planet in the Goldilocks zone of its solar system. Such exoplanets are some of the toughest to find. Since they are smaller than the more easily found gas giants and since they need to orbit closer to their stars to be at the right temperature for life to exist, they can be blocked from sight by their stars' blinding light.

One possible solution to this challenge is a device called the Starshade. Massachusetts Institute of Technology astrophysicist Sara Seager is working with NASA to develop this giant shade, which will be deployed in space to block a star's light. It will give space telescopes a better view of a star's closely orbiting planets. The shade (100 feet, or 30 m, across) is shaped a bit like a sunflower, with a large round center surrounded by petal-like sections with sharp points. Stuart Shaklan, NASA's lead engineer on the Starshade project, explained how the shade will work: "The shape of the petals, when seen from far away, creates a softer edge that causes less bending of light waves. Less light bending means that the starshade shadow is very dark, so the telescope can take images of the planets without being overwhelmed by starlight." The Starshade will travel under its own power and will be positioned to align perfectly with a telescope's line of sight.

To prove that it will work, scientists built a model Starshade and took an image from a telescope on Earth of the bright star Vega. They compared this image with one of the same star taken without the shade. With the shade, the light from the star was one billion times less bright and previously unseen objects and stars close to Vega were visible.

Getting the Starshade to work correctly will be challenging though. Scientists must figure out how the shade will unfold perfectly once in space. The Starshade will also have to stay in exact alignment with a telescope thousands of miles away while the two unconnected pieces of equipment continue orbiting in space. Engineers at NASA's Jet Propulsion Laboratory in California are developing this complicated piece of technology. Once deployed, the shade could help us image smaller Earthlike exoplanets and analyze their atmospheres. If scientists find a biosignature similar to Earth's, it could lead to the discovery of life. Seager is on a mission to make this discovery happen. She says, "I'm devoting the rest of my life to finding other Earths. If there are intelligent aliens, orbiting another planet around a star near to us, all we'll see is a pale blue dot. One little pinprick of life."

6 THE SEARCH CONTINUES

NASA's Transiting Exoplanet Survey Satellite, planned for launch in 2017, will monitor two hundred thousand stars to find exoplanets.

> One of the great questions of all time . . . is whether we are alone in the universe. We live in a time where we can scientifically answer that question.
>
> —*Paul Hertz, director of astrophysics at NASA, 2016*

Exoplanet research is a red-hot field in astronomy. Numerous exoplanet research projects are in progress at both giant telescopes and smaller observatories around the world—and more are on the way.

One exoplanet project is the Gemini Planet Imager (GPI) Exoplanet Survey. It is being conducted by a group of organizations working at the Gemini South Observatory in Chile. The GPI is an advanced adaptive optics system used to make direct images of Jupiter-like exoplanets and their effect on their parent stars' light. Its first exoplanet discovery was made in December 2014, when scientists there imaged 51 Eridani b, a Jupiter-sized exoplanet 100 light-years from Earth with a surface temperature of 800°F (427°C). The survey began in 2014 and will continue to look at six hundred bright stars over several years.

The MEarth project searches for Earthlike planets orbiting around stars that are smaller than our sun. These stars are smaller than our sun. When Earthlike planets transit small stars, they block out a lot of the stars' light, making the transits easier to see than transits across large stars. This survey, run by scientists at the Harvard-Smithsonian Center for Astrophysics, uses two robotically controlled observatories: one in Tucson, Arizona, and the other near La Serena, Chile.

They use arrays to search the skies over both the Northern Hemisphere and Southern Hemisphere. In November 2015, the survey found a rocky planet about 1.2 times the size of Earth that was 39 light-years away. Astronomers will study this planet to better understand the atmosphere of rocky planets outside our solar system.

Another search uses gravitational lensing to find exoplanets. It is the Optical Gravitational Lensing Experiment, run by Polish scientist Andrzej Udalski using a telescope based in Chile. This project found the first three exoplanets identified through microlensing. It studies the same patch of one hundred million stars to detect the bright flashes of light caused by microlensing events.

Using advanced technology, these projects are finding more and more exoplanets every day. Soon even larger eyes will be aimed at the stars. The European Extremely Large Telescope in Chile will have a primary mirror with a diameter of 128 feet (39 m). The Giant Magellan Telescope, also in Chile, will have a primary mirror close to 82 feet (25 m) across. Its images are expected to be ten times clearer than those taken from the Hubble Space Telescope. The Thirty Meter Telescope, planned for Mauna Kea's summit, will have a 98-foot (30 m) primary mirror. These next-generation optical telescopes, expected to go into operation in the 2020s, promise to revolutionize exoplanet research and provide scientists with much greater detail about our universe.

In 2016 the world's largest radio telescope will be completed in Guizhou Province of China. It is the Five-Hundred-Meter Aperture Spherical Radio Telescope (FAST). With a main dish 1,600 feet (500 m) across, it may be able to receive radio emissions from exoplanets the size of Jupiter and larger.

A cutting-edge spectrograph is scheduled for completion in 2019. NASA selected a Pennsylvania State University-led research group to use the device, called NN-Explore Exoplanet Investigations with Doppler Spectroscopy (NEID). NEID will connect to the 11.5-foot (3.5 m) WIYN telescope at Kitt Peak National Observatory in Arizona. Jason Wright, associate professor of astronomy and astrophysics at Penn State, said of the new instrument, "NEID will be more stable than any existing spectrograph, allowing astronomers around the world to make the precise measurements of the motions of nearby, Sun-like stars. Our team will use NEID to discover and measure the orbits of rocky planets at the right distances from their stars to host liquid water on their surfaces."

NEXT-GENERATION MISSIONS

Building upon the successful missions of Kepler and other space telescopes, new planet-hunting telescopes are in the works, and some will soon be ready to launch. NASA's Transiting Exoplanet Survey Satellite (TESS) is planned for launch in 2017. During its two-year mission, it will monitor two hundred thousand stars, looking for transiting exoplanets of all sizes—from Earthlike planets to gas giants. Another NASA project, the Wide Field Infrared Survey Telescope, will also search for exoplanets. It will focus on the direct imaging of exoplanets and is scheduled to launch in the 2020s.

The European Space Agency has some exciting exoplanet missions planned as well. The Characterising Exoplanet Satellite (CHEOPS) mission is set for a 2017 launch. It will detect exoplanets using photometry (the study of stars' luminosity) and will focus on measuring the density of super-Earths and Neptune-sized exoplanets. And in 2024, the ESA's Planetary Transits and Oscillations mission will launch. It will search for Earthlike planets orbiting within the habitable zones of sunlike stars.

The real star in exoplanet research will be launched in 2018. The James Webb Space Telescope will be three times as large as Hubble and one hundred times more powerful. With its 21-foot (6.5 m) mirror and infrared capabilities, Webb will be able to see 13 billion light-years away. Since the light began its journey billions of years ago, the telescope will basically look into our universe's past—back to its beginning.

This telescope will primarily study galaxy, star, and planet formation. Scientists will use Webb to find habitable Earthlike planets, measuring their atmospheres and estimating their daytime temperatures. Jason

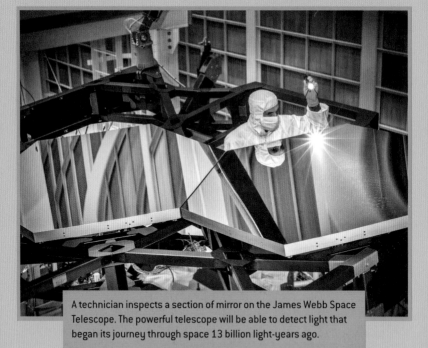

A technician inspects a section of mirror on the James Webb Space Telescope. The powerful telescope will be able to detect light that began its journey through space 13 billion light-years ago.

Kalirai, Webb's project scientist, said of the telescope, "With [Webb] we can measure molecules like carbon dioxide, methane and water vapor in the atmospheres of warm super-Earths orbiting [M dwarf stars]." Webb will work in tandem with TESS, analyzing the planets found by TESS.

CITIZEN SCIENCE: PLANET HUNTING FOR THE PEOPLE

How can you help in the search for new planets? Several options are available. Kepler and other telescopes have gathered vast amounts of astronomical data. Scientists just don't have enough eyes to sort through it all themselves, so they're enlisting the help of citizens. Some volunteers have even found exoplanets.

The Planet Hunters program, run by the Citizen Science Alliance and launched in 2010, asks citizens to help analyze data from the Kepler spacecraft. The goal is to find evidence of an exoplanet's transit across its parent star, indicated by a dip in the star's light during a transit. Volunteers sign up and take tutorials on how to recognize a transit in the data. They then begin analyzing Kepler's data from home computers. The program has nearly three hundred thousand volunteers. They have found thirty exoplanet candidates, several of which have been confirmed as real exoplanets.

The Disk Detective program works to identify stars hidden inside disks of dust. These are where new exoplanets are born. At their home computers, volunteers search through images from NASA's Wide-field Infrared Survey Explorer (WISE) mission. They then classify the images according to certain criteria, such as whether an object in an image is round. Using this information, scientists can choose specific objects to study in depth.

One of the most successful citizen science projects is the SETI@home program, with more than six million volunteers from 226 countries. SETI began the program in 1999. While this project doesn't search for exoplanets, it does search for extraterrestrial broadcasts. Volunteers use their home computers to analyze data from SETI's radio telescopes, searching for signals from space.

SPACE TOURISM •

You might never travel to an exoplanet, but soon you might be able to see space from Earth's orbit. Space tourism is the next big thing in adventure travel. The Virgin Galactic company hopes to be the first commercial spaceline. The company revealed its flagship spaceship, *Unity*, in February 2016. Even with the high price of $250,000 a seat, more than seven hundred people have signed up to travel on *Unity*. "[Unveiling *Unity* was] a significant moment . . . in aviation history," said Dave Mackay, the chief pilot for Virgin Galactic. "This is the vehicle that is going to take many hundreds of regular people into space for the first time."

The SETI Institute operates an array of radio telescopes, all searching the skies for signals from extraterrestrial life. You can join the SETI@home program to help analyze SETI's data.

EXOPLANET BREAKTHROUGHS

While humans may not be able to visit an exoplanet anytime soon, we might be able to send advanced spacecraft to observe and robotic equipment to explore exoplanets. But this will not be easy or quick. It would take a spacecraft traveling at 36,000 miles (58,000 km) per hour seventy-eight thousand years to reach the star nearest to Earth, in the Alpha Centauri star system.

Fuel is also a problem for traveling to other solar systems. Fuel is heavy, and spacecraft can't carry enough to last through an interstellar journey. Close to a star, spacecraft can use solar (star) power as fuel. But when craft get too far from a star, that energy is no longer available. One international science organization, Icarus Interstellar, aims to solve this problem by using nuclear fusion (the combining of two atoms) to power a spacecraft. The group hopes to make interstellar travel a reality by 2100. Nuclear fusion releases enormous amounts of energy. This could provide a spacecraft with enough fuel to reach an exoplanet.

Even if humans never succeed in sending vehicles to exoplanets, as technology improves, scientists will be better able to image exoplanets. We soon may see the outlines of continents and maybe even structures created by alien civilizations. We will also be able to study the atmospheres of Earthlike exoplanets and determine their biosignatures.

We can work to communicate with any life that might exist on exoplanets. And perhaps extraterrestrial civilizations are already listening to us. Humans first began broadcasting radio signals more than one hundred years ago. These signals travel not only around Earth but also out into space in all directions. Maybe an extraterrestrial civilization might receive the signals and send a reply someday.

In less than twenty-five years, scientists have found that our solar system is not unique in the universe. What will the next decades hold for exoplanet science? Scientists will keep looking toward the light, studying all the universe's planetary secrets. It's an exciting time—and there are bound to be many breakthroughs in our understanding of exoplanets and our densely populated universe.

In 2012 the Kepler Space Telescope discovered three small planets orbiting KOI-961, a red dwarf. The three rocky planets are smaller than Earth and orbit close to their star—too close to be in the habitable zone.

SOURCE NOTES

5   Kate Torgovnick May, "Our Night Sky Is Teeming with Exoplanets: Sara Seager on the Hunt for Another Earth at TED2015," *TEDBlog*, March 17, 2015, http://blog.ted.com/sara-seager-on-the-hunt-for-exoplanets-at-ted2015/.

8   Corey S. Powell, "20 Years Later—a Q&A with the First Astronomer to Detect a Planet Orbiting Another Sun," *Scientific American*, October 6, 2015, http://www.scientificamerican.com/article/20-years-later-a-q-a-with-the-first-astronomer-to-detect-a-planet-orbiting-another-sun1/.

8   Michel Mayor and Pierre-Yves Frei, *New Worlds in the Cosmos: The Discovery of Exoplanets* (Cambridge: Cambridge University Press, 2003), 21–22.

11   Ibid., 31.

11   Ibid., 35.

12–13   Ibid., 42.

15   Stephen Hawking, *A Brief History of Time: From the Big Bang to Black Holes* (New York: Bantam Books, 1988), 130.

19   "Life beyond Earth, Part 3: Natalie Batalha," *National Geographic*, film, accessed April 1, 2016, http://video.nationalgeographic.com/video/ng-live/batalha-beyond-earth-lecture-nglive.

31   Neil deGrasse Tyson, "For the Love of Hubble," *Parade*, June 22, 2008, http://www.haydenplanetarium.org/tyson/read/2008/06/22/for-the-love-of-hubble.

39   William Harwood, "How NASA Fixed Hubble's Flawed Vision—and Reputation," *CBS News*, April 22, 2015, http://www.cbsnews.com/news/an-ingenius-fix-for-hubbles-famously-flawed-vision/.

41   NASA, "NASA's Chandra X-ray Observatory Finds Planet That Makes Star Act Deceptively Old," news release, September 16, 2014, http://chandra.harvard.edu/press/14_releases/press_091614.html.

44   NASA, "NASA's Kepler Mission Announces Largest Collection of Planets Ever Discovered," news release, May 10, 2016, http://www.nasa.gov/press-release/nasas-kepler-mission-announces-largest-collection-of-planets-ever-discovered.

45   Mark Zastrow, "Sun's Stroke Keeps Kepler Online," *Nature*, October 21, 2014, http://www.nature.com/news/sun-s-stroke-keeps-kepler-online-1.16195.

45   Alexandra Witze, "Three 'Super-Earth' Exoplanets Seen Orbiting Nearby Star," *Nature*, January 16, 2015, http://www.nature.com/news/three-super-earth-exoplanets-seen-orbiting-nearby-star-1.16740.

47   Hazel Muir, "Ten Years on, a Rich Haul of Planets," *New Scientist* 188, no. 2520 (October 8, 2005): 8–10.

48 "'Astro-Archaeological' Discovery of Replica Solar System with Earth-Sized Planets from the Dawn of Time," University of Birmingham, January 27, 2015, http://www.birmingham.ac.uk/news/latest/2015/01/discovery-of-replica-solar-system-27-01-15.aspx.

48–49 "Astronomers Find the Largest Solar System in the Galaxy," NASA, February 2, 2016, http://planetquest.jpl.nasa.gov/news/247.

49 Devin Powell, "Poof! The Planet Closest to Our Solar System Just Vanished," *National Geographic*, October 29, 2015, http://news.nationalgeographic.com/2015/10/151028-planet-disappears-alpha-centauri-astronomy-science/?utm_source=NatGeocom&utm_medium=Email&utm_content=wild_science_20151108&utm_campaign=Content&utm_rd=652820700.

49–50 Witze, "Three 'Super-Earth' Exoplanets."

50 Andy Bloxham, "Kepler 22b—the 'New Earth'—Could Have Oceans and Continents, Scientists Claim," *Telegraph* (London), December 6, 2011, http://www.telegraph.co.uk/news/science/space/8939138/Kepler-22b-the-new-Earth-could-have-oceans-and-continents-scientists-claim.html.

51 NASA, "NASA's Hubble Telescope Detects 'Sunscreen' Layer on Distant Planet," news release, June 11, 2015, https://www.nasa.gov/press-release/nasa-s-hubble-telescope-detects-sunscreen-layer-on-distant-planet.

52 "NASA's Hubble Reveals Rogue Planetary Orbit for Fomalhaut B," NASA, January 8, 2013, http://www.nasa.gov/mission_pages/hubble/science/rogue-fomalhaut.html.

53 Hazel Muir, "Largest Known Exoplanet Puzzles Astronomers," *New Scientist*, August 6, 2007, https://www.newscientist.com/article/dn12430-largest-known-exoplanet-puzzles-astronomers/.

54 Chris Wickham, "Diamond Planet: '55 Cancri e' Orbits Sun-Like Star 40 Light-Years Away, Astronomers Say," *Huffpost Science*, October 11, 2012, http://www.huffingtonpost.com/2012/10/11/diamond-planet-55-cancri-e_n_1957368.html.

54 "Astronomers Observe Planet with Wild Temperature Swings," NASA, January 28, 2009, http://www.nasa.gov/mission_pages/spitzer/news/spitzer-20090128_prt.htm.

55 Kimm Fesenmaier, "Far beyond Pluto, a Possible Planet Nine Awaits Discovery," NASA, January 20, 2016, http://planetquest.jpl.nasa.gov/news/245.

56 "NASA's Kepler Mission Discovers a World Orbiting Two Stars," NASA, September 15, 2011, http://www.nasa.gov/mission_pages/kepler/news/kepler-16b.html.

57 "Astronomers Image Lowest-Mass Exoplanet around a Sun-like Star," NASA, August 5, 2013, https://www.nasa.gov/content/goddard/astronomers-image-lowest-mass-exoplanet-around-a-sun-like-star.

59 Alissa Greenberg, "Stephen Hawking Endorses New Hunt for Alien Life, Despite Fear of Being 'Conquered and Colonized,'" *Time*, July 22, 2015, http://time.com/3967126/stephen-hawking-seti-extraterrestrial-life-breakthrough/.

59 Carl Sagan, *Pale Blue Dot: A Vision of the Human Future in Space* (New York: Ballantine Books, 1997), 6–7.

67 Mike Wall, "Signs of Alien Life Will Be Found by 2025, NASA's Chief Scientist Predicts," *Space*, April 7, 2015, http://www.space.com/29041-alien-life-evidence-by-2025-nasa.html#sthash.VjozaSt4.G5f5RGEL.dpuf.

69 Joshua Rodriguez, "Flower Power: NASA Reveals Spring Starshade Animation," NASA, March 18, 2014, http://planetquest.jpl.nasa.gov/video/15.

69 May, "Our Night Sky Is Teeming with Exoplanets."

71 Nick Stockton, "NASA's Kepler Just Doubled the Number of Known Exoplanets," *Wired*, May 10, 2016, http://www.wired.com/2016/05/nasas-kepler-mission-just-doubled-number-known-exoplanets/.

73 "NASA Selects Penn State to Lead Next-Generation Planet Finder," Penn State, March 29, 2016, http://science.psu.edu/news-and-events/2016-news/NEID3-2016.

74 Lee Billings, "NASA's Next Space Telescope Promises the Stars—and Planets, Too," *Scientific American*, February 9, 2015, http://www.scientificamerican.com/article/nasa-s-next-space-telescope-promises-the-stars-and-planets-too1/.

75 Rachael Crane and Amanda Barnett, "Virgin Galactic Unveils New Spaceship," *CNN*, February 19, 2016, http://www.cnn.com/2016/02/19/us/virgin-galactic-new-space-plane/.

GLOSSARY

adaptive optics: distorting a telescope's main mirror to adjust for the light-disrupting effects of Earth's atmosphere. Adaptive optics allows astronomers to see starlight more clearly.

astrobiology: the study of life's origins on Earth and the search for it in the universe. Astrobiologists look for exoplanets that might have ingredients for the formation of life, such as water, an atmosphere, and certain gases.

astrophysics: a branch of astronomy that focuses on celestial objects and their properties. Astrophysicists study exoplanets, stars, solar systems, galaxies, and other parts of the universe to understand their formation, makeup, and behavior.

atmosphere: a layer of gases surrounding a planet or other celestial body. Astronomers think that life might exist on some exoplanets with atmospheres because an atmosphere can protect life from dangerous radiation from a star and can also trap the heat and specific gases needed for life to exist.

binary star system: a solar system that contains two stars at its center. Scientists believe that binary star systems are more likely than single star systems to have life because binary systems have larger Goldilocks zones.

biosignature: a substance or substances that indicate that life exists or once existed in a certain place. The substances that comprise Earth's biosignature are chlorophyll, oxygen, and methane.

circumbinary planet: a planet that orbits in a binary star system (a solar system with two stars at its center). Scientists believe that circumbinary planets are more likely to have life than planets orbiting only one star because binary star systems have larger Goldilocks zones than systems with just one star.

cold Jupiter: a planet that has a mass equal to or greater than the mass of Jupiter and that orbits far from its star. Because it orbits far from its star, it is in a cold part of its solar system.

density: a measure of how compact or airy a planet or another object is. A planet that is very dense might be made mostly from rock. A planet that is less dense might be made mostly from gas.

dwarf planet: an object in space that is smaller than a planet but larger than a comet or a meteor. Pluto is a dwarf planet in our solar system.

electromagnetic spectrum: different kinds of light rays arranged according to wavelength, frequency of vibrations, and the amount of energy they contain. On one end of the spectrum are gamma rays, which have the shortest wavelengths, the fastest vibrations, and the most energy. At the other end of the spectrum are radio waves, which have the longest wavelengths, the slowest vibrations, and the least energy. In between the two extremes are X-rays, ultraviolet light, visible light, infrared rays, and microwaves.

elliptical orbit: an oval-shaped orbit around a star. An elliptical orbit might bring a planet very close to its star on one end and very far from its star at the other end.

exoplanet: a planet outside our solar system. Astronomers have identified more than three thousand exoplanets and are studying close to five thousand other objects in space that might be exoplanets.

extraterrestrial: of or from outside of Earth and its atmosphere. The term *extraterrestrial being* refers to life that might exist beyond Earth.

extremophile: a plant, animal, or tiny organisms that can live in an extremely cold, hot, acidic, or salty environment on Earth. Astrobiologists say that if life can exist in harsh environments on Earth, it might also be found in similarly harsh environments on other planets.

galaxy: a system that contains billions of stars and that is held together by gravity. Earth is part of the Milky Way galaxy. Astronomers believe that the universe holds trillions of galaxies.

gas giant: a large planet that has a low density and is made mostly of gases, with an icy core at its center. The gas giants in our solar system are Jupiter, Saturn, Uranus, and Neptune. Astronomers have located many gas giants in other solar systems.

Goldilocks zone: an area within a solar system with temperatures that can sustain liquid water. It is also called a habitable zone. Scientists say that planets that hold water might be able to sustain life.

gravity: an invisible force that attracts two bodies to each other in space or on Earth. Gravity is the force that keeps planets in orbit around stars. Gravity also is the force that causes objects near the surface of Earth to fall to the ground.

habitable zone: an area within a solar system with temperatures that can sustain liquid water. It is also called the Goldilocks zone. Scientists say that planets that hold water might be able to sustain life.

hot Jupiter: a planet that has a mass equal to or greater than the mass of Jupiter and that orbits its star much closer than Jupiter orbits the sun. Because it orbits close to its star, it is in a hot part of its solar system.

mass: the amount of matter in a star, planet, or other object. Two planets of the same size might have very different masses. For instance, a very dense, rocky planet has more mass than a planet of the same size made mostly of gases.

microlensing: when one star passes in front of another star, bending light waves from the source star and causing the light to flare temporarily. If an exoplanet is orbiting the lensing star, the light will briefly flare more intensely. Astronomers look for this extra burst of light to find exoplanets.

nebula: a cloud of gas and dust spinning in interstellar space. Inside a nebula, the spinning gas and dust grow hotter and become the core of a star. The pieces of dust might clump together and form planets orbiting the star.

observatory: a place or building that holds astronomical equipment used to study objects in space. Most observatories are in remote, mountainous regions. There the air holds fewer gases, water droplets, and dust particles to blur images seen through telescopes. Remote areas also have little light pollution to dim incoming starlight.

optical telescope: a telescope that gathers and focuses visible light, producing magnified images of distant objects. Optical telescopes used by astronomers are reflecting telescopes. They use mirrors to gather and focus light.

orbit: the path of an object, such as a planet, as it revolves around another object in space, such as a star

organic: containing carbon, an element that forms the basis of all living things on Earth. The rover *Curiosity* has found carbon molecules on Mars, which leads astronomers to think that the planet could support life or might have in the past.

photometry: the study of a star's luminosity. If astronomers note a drop in a star's luminosity over time, it might mean that a planet is orbiting the star.

pulsar: a rapidly spinning, dying star that emits radiation in the form of radio waves. Gravity from an orbiting planet can make a pulsar wobble and can disrupt the regularity of its radio signals. The irregular signals tell astronomers that a planet might be orbiting the pulsar.

radiation: energy that comes in many varieties and takes the form of waves or tiny particles. Electromagnetic radiation includes gamma rays, X-rays, ultraviolet rays, visible light, infrared rays, microwaves, and radio waves. Astronomers study different kinds of radiation traveling through space to learn about the objects giving off the radiation.

radio telescope: a telescope that gathers and focuses radio waves coming from stars, planets, and other objects in space. Radio telescopes can also detect heat coming from celestial objects and can identify compounds such as water and carbon dioxide.

red giant: a dying star in its last stages of life. When stars become red giants, they expand and engulf the inner planets in their solar systems.

solar system: a system in space held together by gravity, with a star (or stars) at its center and planets or other objects in orbit around the star

spectrograph: an instrument that separates light into its different wavelengths

spectrometer: an instrument that measures the frequency of light waves emitted by a star

transit: in astronomy, when a planet crosses between our line of sight and its star and makes a shadow on the star, blocking its brightness slightly. A shadow on a star is a sign to astronomers that a planet might be transiting the star.

wavelength: the distance from the crest of one wave to the next. On the electromagnetic spectrum, different kinds of light rays have different wavelengths.

SELECTED BIBLIOGRAPHY

Billings, Lee. "NASA's Next Space Telescope Promises the Stars—and Planets, Too." *Scientific American*, February 9, 2015. http://www.scientificamerican.com /article/nasa-s-next-space-telescope-promises-the-stars-and-planets-too1/.

Boss, Alan. *The Crowded Universe: The Search for Living Planets*. New York: Basic Books, 2009.

"Exoplanet Exploration." NASA. Accessed July 25, 2016. http://planetquest.jpl.nasa .gov.

Impey, Chris. *Dreams of Other Worlds: The Amazing Story of Unmanned Space Exploration*. Princeton, NJ: Princeton University Press, 2013.

Mayor, Michel, and Pierre-Yves Frei. *New Worlds in the Cosmos: The Discovery of Exoplanets*. Cambridge: Cambridge University Press, 2003.

"NASA Exoplanet Archive." California Institute of Technology. Accessed July 25, 2016. http://exoplanetarchive.ipac.caltech.edu.

Wolfe, Alexandra. "An Astrophysicist in Search of E.T." *Wall Street Journal*, August 21, 2014. http://www.wsj.com/articles/an-astrophysicist-in-search-of -e-t-1408650066.

FURTHER INFORMATION

BOOKS

Brezina, Corona. *Newly Discovered Planets: Is There Potential for Life?* New York: Rosen, 2016.

Kluger, Jeffrey, and Michael D. Lemonick. *New Frontiers of Space*. New York: Time Books, 2013.

Miller, Ron. *Recentering the Universe: The Radical Theories of Copernicus, Kepler, Galileo, and Newton*. Minneapolis: Twenty-First Century Books, 2014.

——. *Seven Wonders beyond the Solar System*. Minneapolis: Twenty-First Century Books, 2011.

Perryman, Michael. *The Exoplanet Handbook*. New York: Cambridge University Press, 2011.

Sasselov, Dimitar. *The Life of Super-Earths: How the Hunt for Alien Worlds and Artificial Cells Will Revolutionize Life on Our Planet*. New York: Basic Books, 2012.

Seager, Sara. *Exoplanets*. Tucson: University of Arizona Press, 2011.

Toomey, David. *Weird Life: The Search for Life That Is Very, Very Different from Our Own*. New York: W. W. Norton, 2013.

Vakoch, Douglas. *The Drake Equation: Estimating the Prevalence of Extraterrestrial Life through the Ages*. New York: Cambridge University Press, 2015.

Ward, Peter. *A New History of Life: The Radical New Discoveries about the Origins and Evolution of Life on Earth*. New York: Bloomsbury, 2015.

Wittenstein, Vicki Oransky. *Planet Hunter: Geoff Marcy and the Search for Other Earths*. Honesdale, PA: Boyds Mills, 2010.

WEBSITES

Disk Detective
http://www.diskdetective.org
At this website, volunteer planet hunters can search through data to help scientists find debris disks capable of forming planets.

Eyes on Exoplanets
http://eyes.jpl.nasa.gov/eyes-on-exoplanets.html
At this NASA website, you can download a program that allows you to virtually visit known exoplanets. You can zoom in on different planets to find out about their orbital periods, size, and much more.

Planet Hunters
http://www.planethunters.org
This website, sponsored by a project called Zooniverse, allows citizen scientists to help astronomers find exoplanets.

The Search for Another Earth
http://planetquest.jpl.nasa.gov/video/80
This web page from NASA includes a short film about how scientists are searching for Earthlike planets.

Seti@Home
http://setiathome.ssl.berkeley.edu
The SETI Institute is listening for extraterrestrial radio signals. Through the Seti@Home program, you can add your computer power to the search.

Voyager: The Golden Record
http://voyager.jpl.nasa.gov/spacecraft/goldenrec.html
NASA's *Voyager 1* and *Voyager 2* spacecraft carry messages from humankind for any extraterrestrials who might encounter them. At this website, you can listen to the sounds and see the pictures designed to teach other beings about life on Earth.

VIDEOS

Alien Planets Revealed. DVD. Arlington, VA: PBS, 2015. This movie uses animation to bring some of the exoplanets found by the Kepler Space Telescope to life.

"Focusing in on Other Worlds." YouTube video, 57:16. Posted by "NASA," October 19, 2015. https://www.youtube.com/watch?v=vyq7wZrRCHo. In this episode of the What's New in Aerospace series, presented by NASA and the Smithsonian National Air and Space Museum, two experts explain their study of exoplanets and how exoplanet atmospheres may reveal signs of extraterrestrial life.

"How We'll Find Life on Other Planets." Ted Talk video, 5:25, March 2015. http://www.ted.com/talks/aomawa_shields_how_we_ll_find_life_on_other_planets. In this short video, astronomer Aomawa Shields of the University of California–Los Angeles describes the search for life on exoplanets.

"The Search for Another Earth." YouTube video, 18:41. Posted by "NASA Jet Propulsion Laboratory," November 4, 2015. https://www.youtube.com/watch?v=1tUSiWLyN9A. This video covers the history of exoplanet research, starting with speculations about worlds beyond Earth in the sixteenth century and ending with twenty-first-century technology.

"The Search for Planets beyond Our Solar System." TED Talk video, 16:14, March 2015. http://www.ted.com/talks/sara_seager_the_search_for_planets_beyond_our_solar_system. In this TED Talk video, astronomer Sara Seager of the Massachusetts Institute of Technology discusses exoplanets and the prospect of finding another planet like Earth.

"Why Haven't We Found Alien Life?" YouTube video, 12:10. Posted by "PBS Digital Studios," November 5, 2015. https://www.youtube.com/watch?v=cJONS7sqiOo. This episode of PBS's *Space Time* series discusses why Earth is able to sustain life and the possibility of life existing elsewhere in the universe.

INDEX

PHOTO ACKNOWLEDGMENTS

The images in this book are used with the permission of: © iStockphoto.com/
everlite (rocky asteroid background); © sdecoret/Shutterstock.com (green
planetary background); © iStockphoto.com/dem10 (starry sky background);
© Detlev van Ravenswaay/Science Source, p. 4; ESO/M. Kornmesser/Nick
Risinger (CC BY 4.0), p. 6; LAURENT GILLIERON/EPA/Newscom, p. 7; Wikimedia
Commons, p. 10; © Laura Westlund/Independent Picture Service, pp. 13, 23,
25, 27, 34; © Huntington Library/SuperStock, p. 15; NASA/CXC/GSFC/T. Temim
et al., p. 16; © iStockphoto.com/Eerik, p. 18; © ESA, Alfred Vidal-Madjar, NASA,
p. 24; X-ray: NASA/CXC/Univ of Toronto/M.Durant et al; Optical: DSS/Davide De
Martin, p. 28; NASA, pp. 30, 61; © Neelon Crawford - Polar Fine Arts/NSF/Gemini
Observatory/AURA, p. 33; © H. Schweiker/WIYN and NOAO/AURA/NSF/Wikimedia
Commons, p. 36; NASA/ESA/Hubble Heritage Team (STScI/AURA)/J. Hester,
P. Scowen (Arizona State University), p. 40; NASA/CXC/M. Weiss, p. 41; NASA/
Sandra Joseph, Kevin O'Connell, p. 43; NASA Ames/JPL-Caltech/T. Pyle, p. 44;
ESO/M. Kornmesser, p. 46; NASA Ames/JPL-Caltech, p. 50; © Jeffrey Hall,
Lowell Observatory, p. 52; © ESA/Hubble, M. Kornmesser, p. 53; ESO/Tomruen/
nagualdesign (CC BY-SA 4.0), p. 55; NASA/JPL-Caltech/R. Hurt, p. 56; NASA/
Goddard/S. Wiessinge, p. 57; © iStockphoto.com/IakovKalinin, p. 58; NASA/
Dan Burbank, p. 63; © Eye of Science/Science Source, p. 65; NASA/JPL-Caltech/
MSSS, p. 67; NASA/ESA, p. 70; NASA/C. Gunn, p. 74; © Mark Thiessen/Getty
Images, p. 76; NASA/JPL-Caltech, p. 77.

Front cover: © sdecoret/Shutterstock.com.

ABOUT THE AUTHOR

Karen Latchana Kenney is an independent writer and editor in
Minneapolis, Minnesota. She has written books on many subjects,
including how stars form and how human body systems work. Her
award-winning books have received positive and starred reviews in
Booklist, *School Library Connection*, and *School Library Journal*. When
she's not researching and writing books, she loves biking, hiking, and
gazing up at the night sky in northern Minnesota, where the stars are
vividly bright, imagining what kinds of exoplanets orbit each one. Visit
her online at http://latchanakenney.wordpress.com.